# DRY CARGO BARGES
## ON THE
# HUMBER WATERWAYS

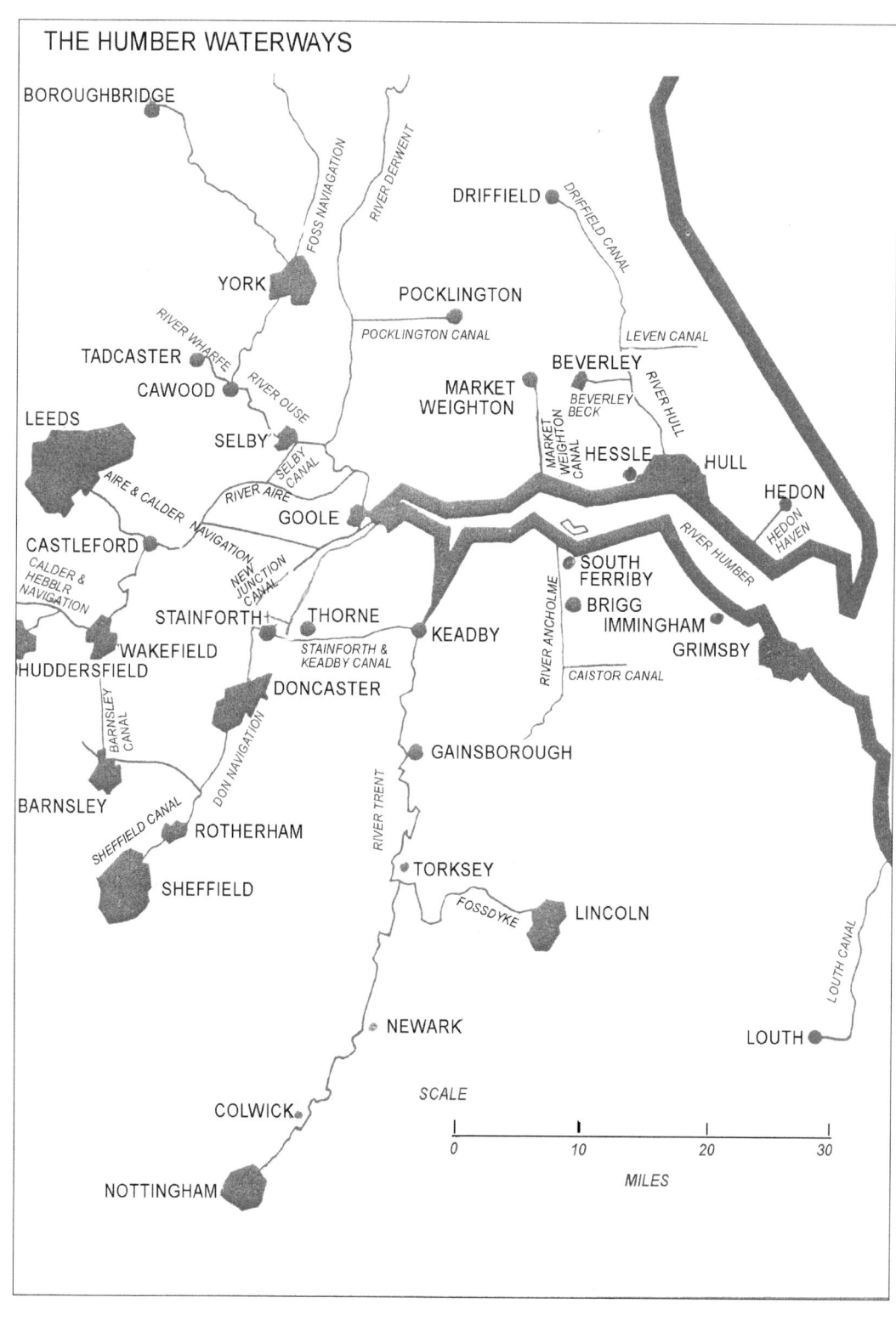

# DRY CARGO BARGES
## ON THE
# HUMBER WATERWAYS

MIKE TAYLOR

TEMPUS

*Frontispiece:* Map of the Humber Inland Waterways. (John Bryce)

First published 2007

Tempus Publishing
Cirencester Road, Chalford,
Stroud, Gloucestershire, GL6 8PE
www.tempus-publishing.com

Tempus Publishing is an imprint of NPI Media Group

© Mike Taylor, 2007

The right of Mike Taylor to be identified as the Author
of this work has been asserted in accordance with the
Copyrights, Designs and Patents Act 1988.

All rights reserved. No part of this book may be reprinted
or reproduced or utilised in any form or by any electronic,
mechanical or other means, now known or hereafter invented,
including photocopying and recording, or in any information
storage or retrieval system, without the permission in writing
from the Publishers.

British Library Cataloguing in Publication Data.
A catalogue record for this book is available from the British Library.

ISBN 978 0 7524 4322 5

Typesetting and origination by NPI Media Group
Printed in Great Britain

# Contents

|  | Acknowledgements | 6 |
|---|---|---|
|  | Introduction | 7 |
| one | By Wind and Tide | 9 |
| two | Pull-Towed Craft | 31 |
| three | Motorised Dumb Vessels | 65 |
| four | Built as SPVs | 91 |
| five | Push-Towed Craft | 115 |

# Acknowledgements

I am grateful to the following individuals for help with the text: Douglas Carey, Henry Dawson, Lawrie Dews, Brian Peeps, Ken Tipton and George Trevethick. Additionally, I am indebted to the owners of several pictures, credited in the relevant captions, for making them available to me.

## Also by Mike Taylor and published by Tempus

*The Calder and Hebble Navigation* (2002)
*The River Trent Navigation* (2000)
*The Sheffield and South Yorkshire Navigation* (2001)
*Shipping on the Humber: The North Bank* (2003)
*Shipping on the Humber: The South Bank* (2003)
*The Yorkshire Ouse Navigation* (2002)
*Tanker Barges on the Humber Waterways* (2006)
*Tugs and Towing Barges on the Humber Waterways* (2006)

Eligible to appear in every chapter in this book except Chapter Four, the steel-built Sheffield size *Loxley* is shown waiting below the closed lower gates of Sprotbrough lock. The motor barge is pushing the barge pens through the lock to take it and its load of Denaby coal to Doncaster power station in 1980. A picture of *Loxley* under sail appeared in *The River Trent Navigation* and it also appears as a motor barge on page 82 of this book. At the time of the photograph its engine was irreparably damaged and the vessel was being used as a push-towed dumb barge.

# Introduction

For centuries, dry cargoes have been carried on the Humber and its tributary rivers. Stone for York Minster was delivered from Doncaster in the fourteenth century and a quarter of a million tons of Anston stone for the Houses of Parliament was brought to London in the mid-nineteenth century, using the Chesterfield Canal for the first part of its journey.

The rivers were steadily made more navigable in order to transport various dry cargoes and, during the Industrial Revolution, locks and canal cuts were constructed on rivers, and complete canals, such as the Chesterfield Canal, Barnsley Canal and Dearne & Dove Canal, were built.

The frontispiece map shows Humber waterways as they were towards the end of the nineteenth century, apart from inclusion of the 1905-built New Junction Canal. Brief histories of the various navigations were given in the relevant volumes listed on page 6 and this book completes a trilogy of books, begun in 2006, relating to the actual cargo-carrying craft on the Humber waterways.

The major dry cargo carried in the region, from the mid-nineteenth century until the 1960s, was coal, both internally on the separate waterways and for export via the Humber ports. Sand, gravel, clay, limestone and bricks have been amongst cargoes loaded and delivered locally, whilst steel, timber, timber products such as paper and strawboard, seeds for crushing, grain and general cargo including foodstuffs, have been amongst imports delivered from the docks onto various waterways. Small amounts of steel, tiles and bricks have been exported in addition to the huge tonnage of coal. Many of these cargoes were transported loose (i.e. in bulk) but others, such as some grain, sugar, steel industry additives and tinned food were carried in sacks or cases, often transhipped to barges in docks at Grimsby, Goole, Immingham and, most importantly, Hull. In the twenty-first century, aggregate from Besthorpe on the river Trent to Whitwood and Ferrybridge on the Aire & Calder Navigation is the region's major dry cargo traffic.

Self-propelled dry cargo craft built until the 1920s were almost invariably designed as towing barges. Like the tugs that were also used to move dumb craft, described in chapters two and five, these were initially steam-powered. Takeover by diesel engines as the major means of propulsion began in earnest during the 1930s. The actual towing units were more fully featured in *Tugs and Towing Barges on the Humber Waterways*.

This book deals with dry cargo barges, both dumb and those powered by diesel engines. The introduction of these engines into craft revolutionised the barging industry. Unpredictable timings depending on a mixture of the vagaries of the elements, horse marines and towing companies were almost eliminated, allowing craft to make faster voyages that were of a more predictable duration.

The chosen chapter headings relate to how the vessels were being operated when the photograph was taken. Unlike later chapters, in the years covered by chapters one and two, the captain of a vessel often had several options open to him when it came to method of movement. For instance, a keel travelling from Sheffield to Beverley could have been bowhauled from Sheffield to a colliery to load, hauled by horse to Mexborough, sailed to Keadby, used a steam tug to travel down the Trent and Humber to Hull, moved up Hull Harbour on the tide and then, perhaps, raised its sail again to reach Beverley Beck, where a horse could have brought it to its berth in the town centre.

Almost all craft depicted were built on the Humber waterways and for several decades around 1900 there were boatyards building wooden craft on every navigation throughout the region. In general, by the Second World War, all the boatbuilders still at work were producing steel vessels and, after SPVs had become the norm in the 1950s, owners of craft then began to increase their carrying capacities by having them lengthened, keeping the yards busy with this and newbuilding.

Reliable pictorial evidence of craft that delivered dry cargoes appears in some early etchings. A few of these have been used in this book, but photographs dating from between the late nineteenth to the early twenty-first century form the bulk of the illustrations used. None has appeared in my other books published by Tempus. Each photograph is credited separately, apart from those taken by me or selected from my collection, which are left uncredited. As in the other two books in this trilogy featuring craft of the Humber's inland waterways, I have interspersed some recollections of men who worked on or with the craft involved amongst the illustrations.

## Notes

A 'barge' is here regarded as a flat-bottomed freight boat, a 'lighter' is a barge used for transporting goods, especially to or from ships and 'dumb' refers to a vessel without an engine.

The First and Second World Wars, 1914–18 and 1939–45 repectively, are often quoted by boatmen and others when asked to date an event. I have also used these terms in captions.

## Maximum Lock Dimensions of some Humber Waterways c.1880

| | |
|---|---|
| Sheffield size | 61½ft x 15½ft |
| Manvers size | 57½ft x 14½ft |
| Lincoln size | 74ft x 15½ft |
| Trent size | 82½ft x 14½ft |
| Upper Trent size | 72ft x 14½ft |
| West Country size | 57½ft x 14ft |
| York (Ouse) size | 90ft x 14½ft |

Lock sizes were crucial in determining the dimensions of craft that were able to trade on a particular waterway and are quoted in the above table and throughout the book to the nearest ½ft.

The Aire & Calder Navigation Company adopted a policy of increasing the dimensions of its locks throughout its existence and dimensions were never critical on this waterway.

On the Sheffield & South Yorkshire Navigation, the length of Doncaster lock was increased in 1910, Bramwith lock in 1932 and Long Sandall lock in 1959. Above Doncaster, the locks remained Sheffield size until the improvements of the early 1980s to locks up to Rotherham.

New and bigger Trent Navigation locks, at least 190ft x 30ft, were built between 1911 and 1952.

Locks at the lower end of the Calder & Hebble Navigation were lengthened from their original West Country size in 1865, allowing Sheffield size craft to reach British Oak staithe.

A new lock was built at Naburn on the Ouse in 1888 with dimensions of 159ft x 26ft, allowing much larger craft to reach York, though Castle Mills lock, at the entrance to the city's Foss Navigation, was rebuilt in 1889 to dimensions of only 97ft x 18½ft.

The following abbreviations have been used:
| | |
|---|---|
| A&CNC | Aire & Calder Navigation Co. |
| BACAT | Barge Aboard CATamaran |
| BOCM | British Oil & Cake Mills |
| BTC | British Transport Commission (1953–1962) |
| BWB | British Waterways Board, later British Waterways (1963–2007), became Aquantis in 2007 |
| C&HNC | Calder & Hebble Navigation Co. |
| D&IWE | Docks & Inland Waterways Executive (1948–1952) |
| LASH | Lighter Aboard SHip |
| L&LCC | Leeds & Liverpool Canal Co. |
| S&SYNC | Sheffield & South Yorkshire Navigation Co. |
| SPV | Self-Propelled Vessel |
| TNC | Trent Navigation Co. |
| YDDC | Yorkshire Dry Dock Co. |

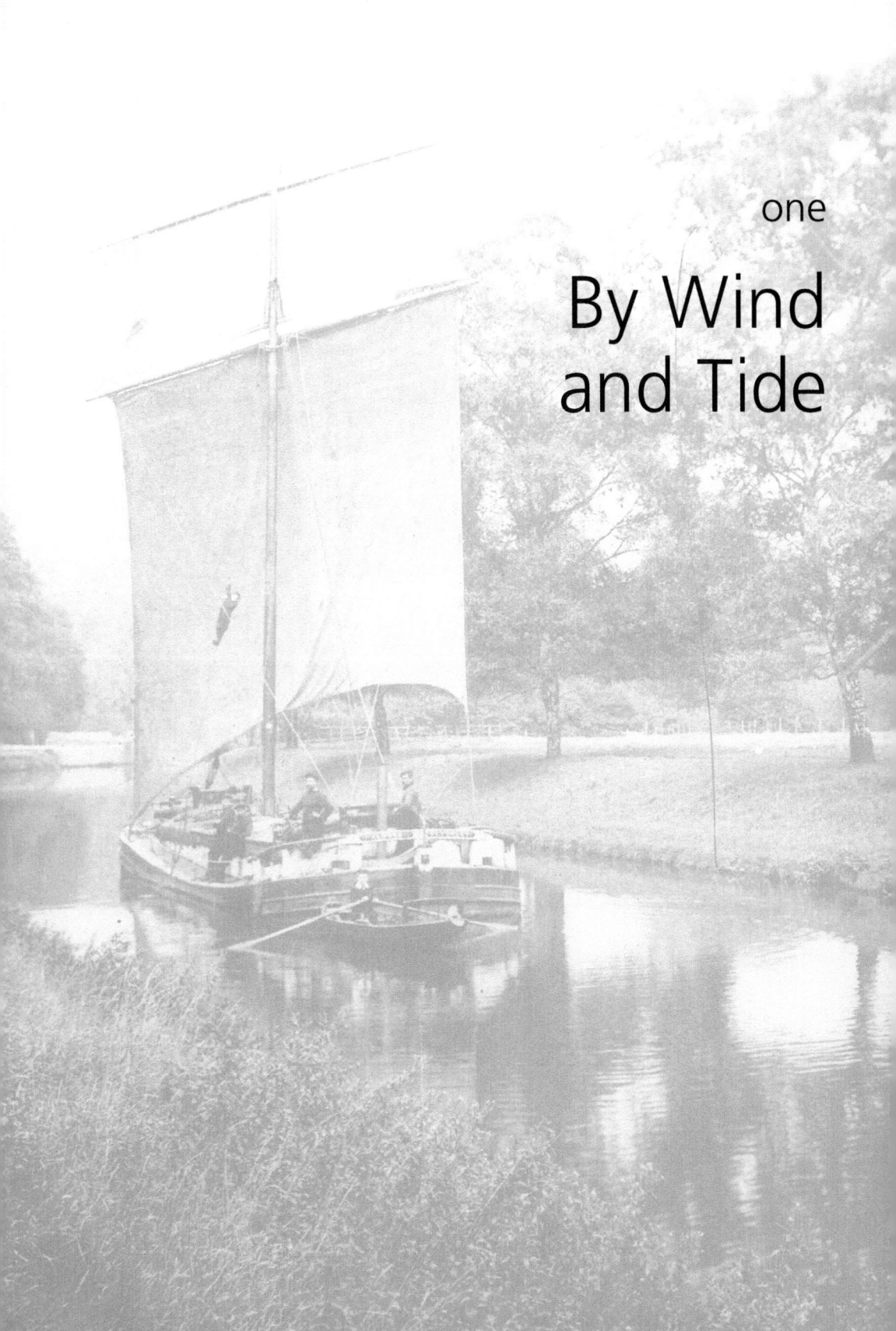

one

# By Wind and Tide

Humber keels and sloops are the most widely known sailing craft of the region and served the Humber's inland waterways for decades. Basically, the two types differed only in their sailing rig and were readily interconverted. Both were fitted with leeboards on each side of the vessel which, when lowered on the wider rivers, prevented it from being blown sideways. Keels operated throughout the nineteenth century and earlier and were more suited to the shallower, straighter canals where the overhanging parts of a sloop's sails could cause problems. They were prevalent until the Second World War, most notably on the S&SYN. Sloops were less common and came onto the scene later than keels. They also finished at about the same time and were more at home on the wider tidal rivers of the region, being mainly based at Hull and on the south bank of the Humber, most notably at Barton-on-Humber. Cross-Humber work was their major activity. Local billyboys and visiting spritsail barges from the Thames and south-east England seaports also formed a smaller part of the sailing scene. There were several craft that, on occasions, raised an improvised sail approximating in shape to – but smaller than – a keel's mainsail.

Sailing craft relied on the tides for assistance whenever possible, but exclusive use of the tidal flow for movement of dumb vessels was extremely important on the river Hull until the 1970s. Similarly, tidal power alone could be used for craft to cross between north and south banks of the Humber and to move on the rivers Trent and Ouse.

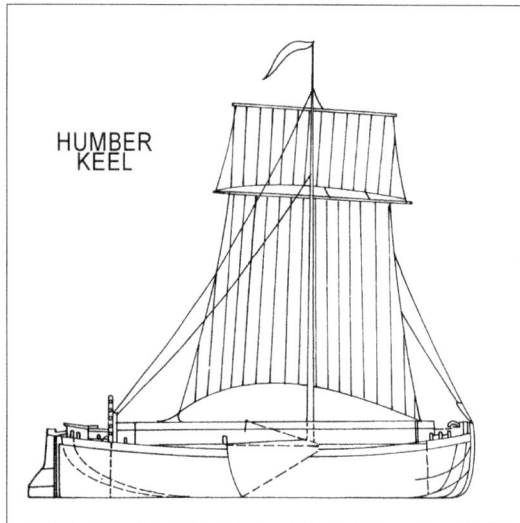 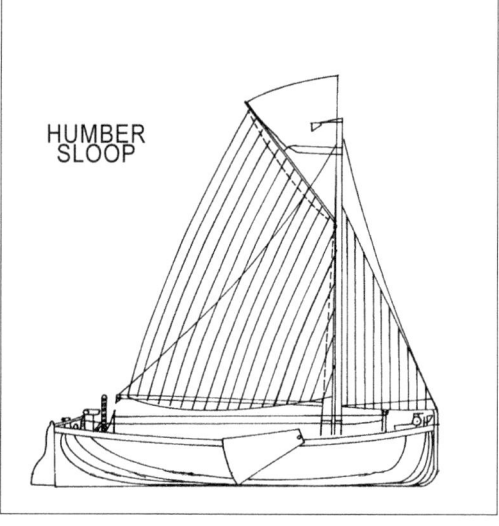

The sailing rigs of keels and sloops are shown above. Keels (mainyard suspended symmetrically from the mast) and sloops (mainsail boom projecting out of the confines of the vessel and foresail evident) can be identified even when their sails are furled.

The laden Sheffield size keel, *Alboro*, with both mainsail and topsail set and a child partway up the rigging, is heading towards Doncaster as it comes down the S&SYN's Sprotbrough cut on this posed picture.

*Left:* The narrow channel above the road bridge over Sprotbrough cut is shown before its widening in 1908, just as a keel, with mainsail set, comes down the S&SYN.

*Below:* An etching from the 1850s showing a keel and sea-going vessel at Edmund Main colliery, near Barnsley on the Worsbrough arm of the D&DC, which the S&SYNC closed in 1906 because of mining subsidence, shortly after assuming responsibility for it in 1895. (John Goodchild collection)

*Above:* A keel with both mainsail and topsail raised approaches Thorne Waterside as it comes down the river Don. After 1939, access to this part of the navigation was only via the Dutch River, entered at Goole. The lock from the S&SYN at Stainforth, which would have been used by this keel, has closed.

*Right:* A keel spilling wind from its mainsail as it negotiates Stainforth high-level swing bridge whilst coming down the S&SYN. The bridge was replaced by a fixed span in 1948.

*Above:* Keels with mainsails set passing each other close to Watsons' shipyard on the river Trent at Gainsborough in 1899.

*Left:* A loaded keel, with its cog boat in tow, sailing on the Fossdyke in the 1930s.

*Opposite above:* Keels frozen in on the Fossdyke in Lincoln during the winter of 1940. (*Lincolnshire Echo*)

*Opposite below:* Keels with sails furled (and in some cases also lifted to avoid obstructing the discharge of their cargoes) moored in Lincoln's Brayford in the 1900s.

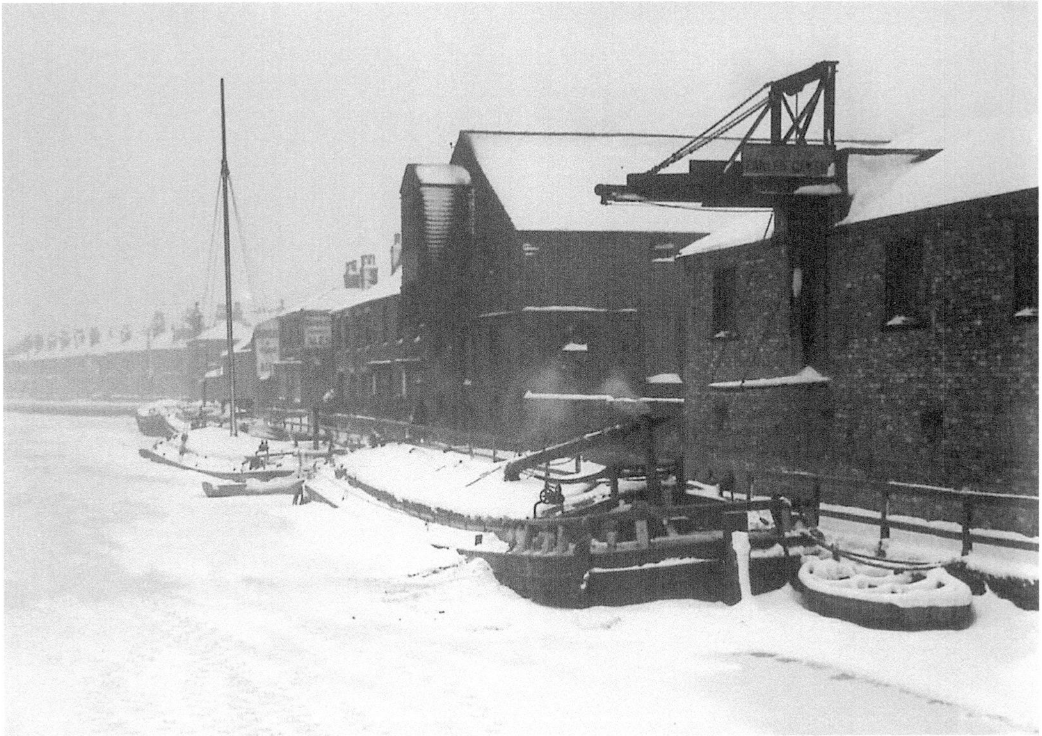

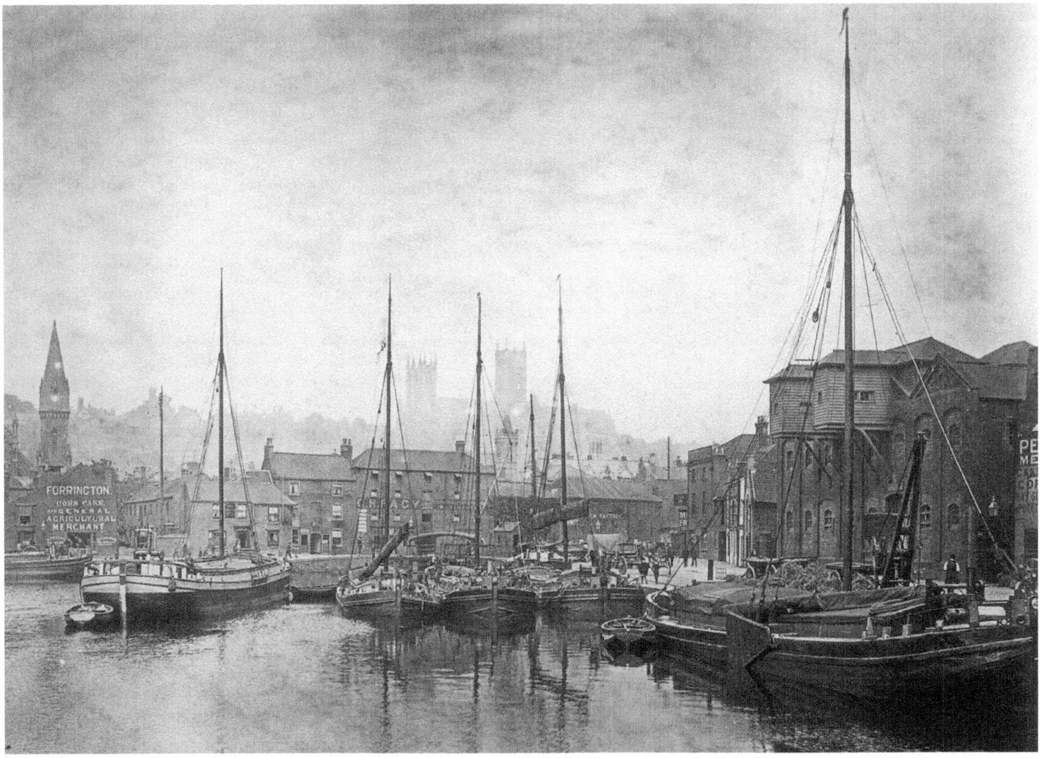
FORRINGTON
AGRICULTURAL
MERCHANT

*Above:* An etching from the 1840s showing shallow-draughted keels discharging their cargoes near Bardney railway station on the river Witham between Lincoln and Boston. (Pat Jones collection)

*Below:* Albert Chester's loaded Sheffield size steel keel, *Voluta*, Warrens-built in 1909, sailing up the Ancholme Navigation in 1932.

*Above:* Four light keels sailing down the Humber to load in one of Hull's eastern docks after coaling trawlers in the fish docks.

*Right:* With both topsail and mainsail set, the keel *Willie* and its captain pose on the Driffield Canal.

Looking up the river Aire towards Leeds Bridge, this etching from the 1820s shows the sailing craft, two of which seem to be sea-going vessels, that reached the city before the introduction of the A&CNC's merchandise towing service. (John Goodchild collection)

A keel waiting to discharge timber at the Ouse's Marygate landing in York.

Wooden keels, the outside one carvel-built (abutted planks) and its neighbour clinker-built (overlapping planks), waiting for attention at the boatyard below York's Skeldergate Bridge over the Ouse in the 1900s.

Dating from the 1880s, this postcard view taken on York's river Foss shows sailing craft moored above Castle Mills lock.

Built for themselves by Furley & Co. at Gainsborough in 1858, the wooden sloop *Bee* eventually became one of Stamps' cross-Humber market boats and is shown here, with its cog boat in tow, in that capacity. The vessel was derigged in 1903 to become a lighter in Hull Docks. (Hull Maritime Museum)

*Right:* James Barraclough & Co.'s 68ft x 16ft steel sloop *Phyllis*, built in 1909 by Warrens of New Holland, shown here participating in the 1928 Barton sloop regatta. (Humber Keel & Sloop Preservation Society)

*Below:* A sloop with mainsail partly lowered enters the river Hull from the Humber. (Humber Keel & Sloop Preservation Society)

A keel, with sails furled and a bagged cargo being transferred to or from a horse-drawn dray, lies at Hull's Horsewash where the Barton Market boats loaded and discharged. A sloop beyond, with mainsail set, heads out of the river Hull into the Humber in the 1930s.

The only wooden vessel in John Richardson & Son's fleet of Market Weighton Canal 'coal in/bricks out' sloops, the 65ft x 14½ft *Faxfleet* passes Barton Ness jetty on the Humber in 1928. The vessel was built by Collingham Brothers of Goole in 1902 for Henry Williamson of Broomfleet, the brickmakers, who sold it to Richardsons in 1922. (Humber Keel & Sloop Preservation Society)

A sloop heading up the Trent is featured in this view of Morton Corner, near Gainsborough.

George H. Anderton & Co, fertiliser manufacturers of Howdendyke, owned a small fleet of sea-going sloops which carried imports from Hull to their Ouse-side factory and delivered exports to ports on the Wash. Their 62ft x 17½ft carvel-built wooden sloop *Hydro*, built by William Causley in 1897, also at Howdendyke, is shown with mainsail, foresail, bowsail, pre-bowsail and topsail set, heading up the Ouse in the early 1930s. (Humber Keel & Sloop Preservation Society)

The possible obstruction caused by a sloop's boom can appreciated in this photograph of J.J. Tomlinson's Sheffield size *Clarence T*, Warrens-built in 1925, discharging a cargo at the A&CN's Leeds Terminus.

The sloop in the foreground of this picture of craft in Grimsby's Alexandra Dock has its boom fastened well out of the way to give access to its cargo hold.

A loaded wooden keel, probably unfit for sailing on the Humber, using a small mast and sail on the S&SYN to come down Sprotbrough cut towards the lock in the 1930s. (Bob May collection)

The spritsail barge *Lord Rosebery* receiving attention at Clapsons' boatyard inside Barton Haven in the 1930s.

Many of the spritsail barges entering the Humber waterways came to collect coal, usually loaded on the Trent at Keadby, as *Leonard Piper* is waiting here to do in the 1920s.

*Right:* Humber billyboys were round-stemmed, round-sterned sailing craft built with bulwarks to make them more sea-worthy than keels or sloops. Many were rigged both fore and aft and, until they ceased trading in the 1910s, worked as coasters based at Knottingley on the river Aire, as well as at Goole and Hull. The wooden billyboy, *Beverley*, built in Holland in 1861, is shown moored in Hull Harbour in the late nineteenth century when owned by a Beverley carrier. (Hull Maritime Museum)

*Below:* Tugs and lighters are moored below Hull's 1888-built Drypool Bridge in the 1930s (the current bridge dates from 1961). An enormous number of dumb craft, loaded with cargoes for upriver premises, were brought to this spot by tug and left to make their own ways to their destinations.

*Above:* After being towed into the mouth of the river Hull (Hull Harbour), craft had to turn to go upriver stern-first with the tide. Movement was possible three or four hours before high water. Gilyott & Scott's 71ft x 19ft steel lighter *Coly*, built by Cochrane & Sons of Selby in 1924, is shown in 1978 turning above Drypool Bridge, with the helmsman giving assistance using a broom!

*Left:* As it moves upriver, the lighter is steered by the helmsman. This ability to steer is provided by the man shown at the bows with a winch that he uses to raise and lower a 56lb mudweight fastened to a 30ft chain, allowing it to drag along the river bed to ensure that the lighter moves slower than the tidal current and to give the vessel steerage.

*Opposite above:* A photograph taken from one lighter showing two others slowly drifting stern-first up the river Hull with the tide. Craft never carried navigation lights or life jackets.

*Below:* Arrival of the lighters at their destination in Hull Harbour has precipitated more vigorous activity amongst the crew as craft are tied up, the tillers removed and bicycles lifted ashore.

The dumb barge *Edward*, carrying coal from the Barnsley Canal to Beverley, is shown moving stern-first up the river Hull at Stoneferry with assistance from three crew members wielding stowers, probably because tides were small at the time.

Chesterfield Canal narrowboats (cuckoos) occasionally ventured onto the tidal river Trent at West Stockwith and voyaged upriver to Gainsborough or Torksey. Two of these may be seen in the foreground, off the Gainsborough bank, acting as stands for spectators of the local watersports. The further vessel has a Union Jack atop its raised mast and, coming upriver with the tide, would probably have been rowed and may have raised a small sail if the wind was favourable. Returning to Stockwith, the vessels would run with the tide, using the oars to keep on course.

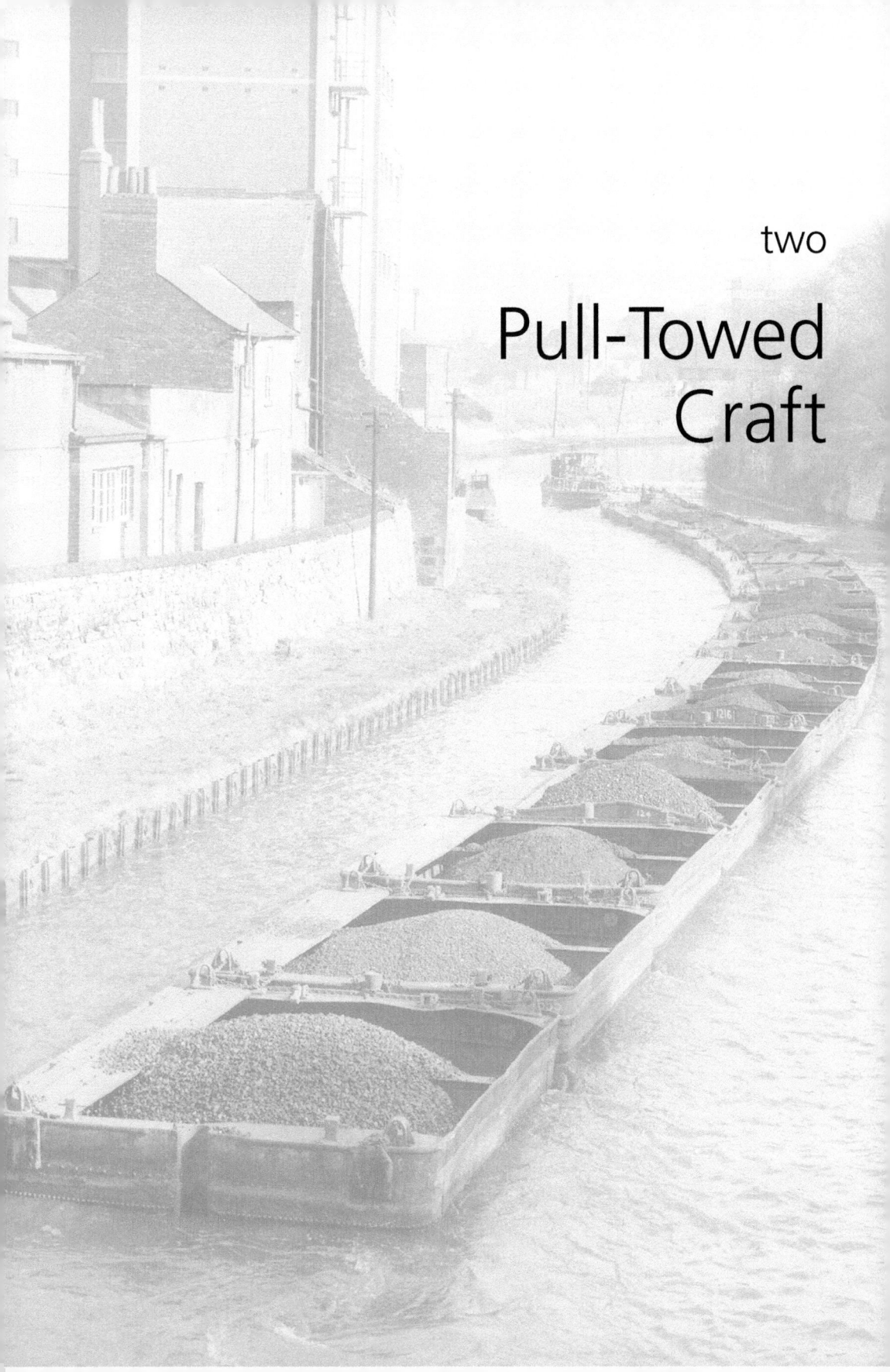

two

# Pull-Towed Craft

Pull-towing by man, horse, tug or towing barge could all once be seen on the Humber waterways. Bowhauling, involving movement of a vessel at the end of a rope by human power, was only occasionally practised in the days of sail and, even then, usually used for distances of no more than a few miles, except by impecunious captains who had no options. Horses were almost invariably used on the internal traffic on every navigation until the 1920s. Keels and sloops travelling on the upper reaches of a waterway also often used this means of movement. The S&SYN was especially busy and all keels bound for Rotherham or Sheffield used horses above Mexborough, due to the many low bridges which made the retention of mast and sails a time-consuming handicap. Horse haulage also persisted on other navigations, such as the Barnsley Canal and C&HN, until the coming of motorised craft in the 1930s. Pull-towing, initially by steam-powered tugs and towing barges and later by diesel-engined craft, has been a feature of the local waterways since the mid-nineteenth century. On tidal rivers, towing craft based at Hull, Nottingham, Goole, Selby and York hauled dumb craft that may have sailed, used the tide or been hauled by horse before or after the tow. The A&CN saw extensive pull-towing, and both a merchandise-towing service for by-traders' craft and the famous Tom Puddings (compartment boat operation) used A&CNC tugs and towing barges. A few Leeds-based companies also towed their craft, usually loaded with coal, up to and through the city, by horse until the 1920s and later by their own tugs.

Some wooden craft are shown at the boatyards where they were built. All these wood-specialists, except Stanilands of Thorne and Ledgard Bridge yard at Mirfield, ceased trading during the first half of the twentieth century steel as craft became the norm.

*Left:* The A&CNC's well-patronised steam towing service ensured that there was not as large a demand for horse haulage as there could have been on such a busy waterway. What little horse-haulage that did exist lasted here until the 1940s. On river navigations such as the A&CN and S&SYN, where the towpath changed banks, facilities were provided to ferry horses across river. A horse and its handler are shown being sculled across at Fryston. (Jack Hulme)

*Opposite above:* The launch of the 60ft x 14ft wooden Leeds & Liverpool 'shortboat' *Self Help* at Garlick's Knottingley boatyard in 1900 is illustrated. Hauled by horse, the vessel would deliver coal from collieries on the A&CN to wharves on the L&LC above Leeds. This boatyard became part of Harkers' yard in the 1920s. (Ron Gosney collection)

*Opposite below:* The Leeds & Liverpool Canal (L&LC) took some of the A&CN's traffic westwards above Leeds. The short Bradford Canal left the L&LC at Shipley and the Pearson family's *Harry* poses with its towing horse in the lower lock of the Spinkhill pair, half a mile from the city's canal terminus.

The C&HN is essentially a continuation of the A&CN's Wakefield branch, further into West Yorkshire. Its waterway traffic was almost all horse-hauled until the 1930s. An A&CNC flyboat, its crew and towing horse plus handler pose for the camera in the lower of Double locks, near Dewsbury, in the 1930s.

*Opposite above:* Whilst its towing horse waits patiently, *William* pens down Long Lees lock on the C&HN in the 1940s, en route to collect another load of coal for Sowerby Bridge gasworks.

*Opposite below:* Leading off the A&CNC's Wakefield Branch like the C&HN, the Barnsley Canal saw horse-drawn traffic to its end in the mid-twentieth century. With its towing horse feeding on the move, a barge, probably loaded with coal, leaves the fifth lock down as it descends the Walton flight.

*Left:* One of Hanleys' Sheffield size keels, *Danum*, illustrates a vessel being bowhauled. The picture was taken near Crowle on the S&SYN and appears to have been posed, with the procedure being unnecessary as the keel's sails seem to be catching the wind.

*Below:* This late nineteenth-century photograph shows Sheffield Basin, before construction of the Straddle Warehouse, full of wooden craft that will all have been brought to the city by horse.

*Above:* There were facilities for a keel to leave its mast and sails in safe keeping on the S&SYN at Mexborough, Doncaster, Stainforth and Keadby, as it transferred to horse haulage to voyage further up the S&SYN. This postcard view shows the masting crane and stored masts at Stainforth.

*Below:* A horse and horse marine prepare to resume towing a laden vessel up the S&SYN after penning up one of the locks, probably at Kilnhurst.

30th October, 1936.

### REPORT BY CAPTAIN EMERSON
### KEEL "BEECLIFFE".

Horse slipped on edge of hollow (made by horses, and not filled up) in Towing Path near Roundwood Rack on Wednesday the 28th October and fell on its side. - No sign of injury and hauled boat to Tinsley.

When put in stable refused to eat or drink and although attended by vet died to-day 30th October.

Purchased for £12. two weeks ago.

Emerson puts it down to injury received when it fell and asks if you can assist him in any way, as he has no money to buy another horse. He did not suggest that we were liable. It was his own horse and he was leading it himself.

Witnessed by F. Brammer.

Many claims relating to injury or death of a horse were received by the S&SYNC. The above is a copy of the summary – by the foreman of the S&SYNC's Tinsley Section – of details handed to him by the owner of an unfortunate horse. The summary was then sent by Mr W.H. Pryce, the S&SYNC's General Manager, to the company's insurers with the note that the captain of *Beecliffe* was not claiming the full value of the horse, but was merely asking for some assistance in purchasing another animal. The vet's certificate, also included with the note, indicated that peritonitis following rupture of its caecum was the cause of death.

A pencilled note indicating that £4 was paid to the captain closes the file of notes on the incident.

## Jim Rownsley, Horse Marine

Dad left the coal mines in 1924 and set up as a horse marine based here on the canal at Mexborough. Most craft sailing from Hull to Rotherham or Sheffield left their mast and sails here and changed to horse power, though some did this at Keadby, Stainforth or Doncaster. I can remember going with him many times in the holidays and when I left school in 1929, he bought me a horse and I worked on the navigation for about ten years until horses finished before the war.

I picked up customers by letter or telegram from a captain leaving Hull, casually from captains I passed on the canal, or, most often, by telephone to Mexborough Top lock. The lock keeper then delivered the captain's message to me personally, at home.

One end of the 60-yard long, 1½in-circumference cotton hauling line was usually fastened to a sturdy piece of timber, such as a pit prop, stepped in the barge's lutchet, unless the mast was still aboard, when it would be fixed to the forestays close to the lutchet. The other end was connected to a hook on the horse's cobblestick or singletree. Leaving a lock, with the horse leaning into its collar, I walked backwards until there was no risk of the hauling line fouling anything and then let out more line as the vessel re-entered the river section.

My busiest ever week was in 1935. One Sunday, Herbert Green rang up for a tow from Doncaster, with deals for Sheffield. I left here at one o'clock Monday morning, tramped to Doncaster and then hauled him to Sheffield Basin. I got back here about two o' clock on Tuesday morning. I had one already booked from Denaby to Keadby for later that morning and, as soon as I'd finished with him I got another that had come up on the tide for Rotherham. After that, I got back home on Thursday afternoon with an order next day fom Roundwood to Doncaster.

Keadby to Sheffield took me between thirty and thirty-six hours of movement, sleeping in lock lobbies or aboard the keel. When tramping back, I came by the shortest route, usually overland, by road, missing out the horse ferries at Kilnhurst and Eastwood, where the towpath changed sides as canal and river met. Horses fed on the move and I fed mine with a mixture of bran, hay choppings and split maize. I was supposed to be fed by the captain of the keel I was hauling and the food ranged from excellent to miserable. There were stables at many places along the navigation where the horse could rest overnight and blacksmiths at all settlements we went through, including three at Mexborough.

The blacksmith was my major expense. Four new shoes were needed every six weeks and the previous six week's natural growth was then cut away from each hoof. If a horse had bad joints, leather or rubber would be put between its hooves and shoes to act as a cushion. Frost nails, which stuck out below the shoe to help the horse keep its footing in snow and ice, were often fitted in winter and, probably once a year, the animal's teeth would need filing to enable it to eat better. I looked after my horse and so did the majority of the horse marines but there were a few exceptions!

During the 1930s, new motor barges were built and engines were being fitted into keels. All these motor barges could also do the work of a horse and tow a dumb barge, if necessary, and the skipper did not have to feed a horse marine! This killed off horse haulage of vessels.

Jim Rownsley's horse in 1934, waiting at Sprotbrough lock.

Jim Rownsley's father is shown handling the horse at Conisbrough lock as it prepares to tow Robinsons' coal-laden *Annie Maud* down the S&SYN on its voyage to Hull. The Sheffield size wooden keel would have retrieved its mast at Mexborough less than an hour before.

The Hewitt family aboard their horse-drawn cuckoo *Mavis* on the Chesterfield Canal, near Drakeholes Tunnel. *Mavis* regularly rowed/sailed to Lincoln (see page 30) with household coal.

Boat trips behind a horse were popular throughout the Humber's rivers and canals at one time. Retford Wesleyans are shown boarding Chesterfield Canal cuckoos in 1899 prior to a trip to Drakeholes.

*Above:* Craft are waiting in Goole's Barge Dock in the 1900s for a tow by one of the A&CN's Merchandise tugs to either Leeds or Wakefield.

*Left:* Several of the craft waiting at Goole would have loaded cargoes overside from ships in Hull Docks as this vessel is doing here. They would then come up to Goole behind one of the Goole & Hull Steam Towing Co.'s tugs.

The A&CNC's Merchandise Towing Service, headed by a steam towing barge, prepares to negotiate the Great North Road bridge at Ferrybridge in 1931 and head up the 'five-mile pond' towards Castleford past Ferrybridge 'A' power station.

An A&CNC Merchandise Tow pauses on the river Aire above Ferrybridge flood lock in the 1920s whilst returning to Goole. Six unladen craft are being hauled by a steam towing barge. (Ron Gosney collection)

*Above:* The 1949 launch at Harkers of the D&IWE's 72ft x 15½ft dumb barge *I.W.N.E. No.1*, designed to be towed by the new diesel-powered towing barges that were then being built to replace the Merchandise steam tugs.

*Left:* Loaded and light trains of the famous 20ft x 15ft, 9ft-deep Tom Puddings passing each other at Castleford in the early 1950s when steam tugs were nearing replacement by newly built diesel tugs.

*Right:* Pans were loaded at colliery staithes on the A&CN for over a century and at Hatfield colliery on the S&SYN from 1932. Lorry-fed staithes at Castleford, Doncaster and Wakefield (shown here with Fall Ings lock in view) were used to load coal from collieries away from the waterside. (BW)

*Below:* Pans were occasionally shunted using human energy as shown here at Doncaster loading staithe.

*Opposite:* One of the eight diesel tugs, built in the 1950s to replace the steam units, hauls its train of loaded puddings through Knottingley in 1967, bound for Goole. (Norman Burnitt)

*Right:* The tipping of a pudding's contents into the hold of a ship is shown at No.3 hoist in Goole's Aldam Dock, one of the five hoists which were sited at Goole. Coal trimmers are standing on the ship's cargo. (Norman Burnitt)

*Below:* For decades around the turn of the nineteenth century, coal was also exported from Goole by sea-going barges such as the 350-ton capacity *Queen of the Bay*, shown here in Goole docks. Owned by the Goole & Hull Steam Towing Co., the vessel made frequent voyages to the Thames, towed by the company's steam tug *Goole No.10*.

Hargreaves' tug-hauled wooden dumb barges, the 70ft x 15½ft *Hilda* and 60ft x 14½ft *Joan*, discharging coal at their East Street wharf on the river Aire at Leeds in 1955. Both craft were built at Riders' yard, near the L&LC's Junction lock in Leeds. (Hargreaves)

*Opposite above:* Hargreaves delivered huge quantities of coal in West Yorkshire and this 1946 photograph, taken from Brotherton church, shows their steam tug *Audrey* hauling three barges loaded with coal downriver towards Ferrybridge 'A' power station ('B' and 'C' stations had not been built at this time). (Hargreaves)

*Opposite below:* Hargreaves' 200-ton capacity, 80ft x 16½ft dumb barge *Doreen* being turned on the river Aire outside Ferrybridge 'A' power station in the 1940s by *Audrey*, prior to heading back upriver to load another cargo of coal. (Hargreaves)

*Left:* Both Leeds Industrial Co-operative Society and Leeds Corporation Electricity Department had their own fleet of barges which brought coal from collieries sited alongside the A&CN to the city. These craft were initially hauled by horse and later by tugs. Some of the former's tugs and dumb barges are shown moored outside their river Aire depot in the late 1960s.

*Below:* There was no towpath through Leeds along the river Aire and craft used either a tug service or the cheaper option of poling the vessel between Leeds lock on the A&CN and River lock, at the eastern end of the L&LC. Preferably, this was done with the current as shown on this early twentieth-century view looking downstream. The vessel, with a woman at the tiller, is passing the city's terminus of the A&CNC's Merchandise Towing Service (on the right).

This aerial view from 1955 shows a loaded tanker barge heading for Leeds about to pass a light motor-dumb barge pull-tow heading down the A&CN at Stourton. The dumb vessel is fastened close-up to the tug for ease of handling. (BWB)

The loaded dumb barge at anchor between Selby Railway swing bridge and the shipyard, near the entrance to the Selby Canal, is probably waiting for one of the City of York tugs to enable it to complete its voyage up the Ouse to York, perhaps carrying coal from the West Riding of Yorkshire.

*Left:* The 97ft x 18½ft dumb barge, *Blow's Victoria*, built by Selby Shipbuilding & Engineering Co. in 1905 as *Leetham's Victoria*, is shown discharging a bagged cargo via a hoist into Rowntree's (formerly Leetham's) warehouse on York's river Foss in the 1940s. The vessel was purchased by Nelson Blow and renamed in 1929.

*Below:* The 97ft x 19ft *Selby Taurus* outside Dunstons' yard shortly after completion there in 1921. The dumb vessel, owned by Selby oil mills and based there, made many voyages behind tugs to and from Hull Docks.

*Opposite above:* The 79½ft x 17½ft dumb lighter *Blow's Albert* outside Scarrs' yard at Hessle where it was completed in 1925 to be used by Nelson Blow on his cross-Humber service between Hull and Grimsby.

*Below:* Gilyott & Scott's 71ft x 19ft steel lighter *Torcha*, Dunston-built in 1928, being hauled to its berth in Hull's King George Dock in 1979 by a tug from which the lightermen had begged a 'pull'. Dumb craft used tugs to get to and from Hull Docks but inland waterway tugs rarely entered the docks and lighters were generally moved within a dock by their crews using ropes and windlass. The mudweight may be seen hanging from the lighter's bow.

The 75ft x 19ft wooden lighter *Whitakers No.49* outside the yard of Staniland & Co. of Thorne where the vessel was built in 1922. (Whitakers)

In Hull's Alexandra Dock, ships often moored projecting out into the dock with their sterns against the wall, thus facilitating loading their cargoes 'overside' into inland waterway craft on each side of them. Barges are shown in the early 1900s, receiving seeds by the 'rip and tip' method from ships moored in this manner, via a chute.

Dumb inland waterway craft loading and waiting to load grain in the 1930s at the 1919-built silo in Hull's King George Dock. Eight vessels could be loaded simultaneously; four on the outside with bulk wheat (via sloping chutes) and four inside with bagged wheat (via vertical drops).

These concrete lighters, moored in Hull's Victoria Dock in 1947, were built for the Admiralty, as an emergency measure, during the Second World War. Several were used as part of the river Trent bank at Morton, near Gainsborough, when it was reconstructed after the river breached its banks in the late 1940s. (*Hull Daily Mail*)

Two spritsail barges, *Britannic* amd *Success*, and two Sheffield size keels, *Nar* and *Westcliffe*, under tow in the Trent at Keadby in the 1930s. The tug has again turned its tow 'head-to-tide' for ease of control.

*Opposite above:* Dumb craft waiting in the 1940s for the entrance lock gates to open so that they can leave Hull's Alexandra Dock for the Humber, where they will be collected by tugs and taken to their destinations on the local inland waterways.

*Opposite below:* A sloop sails downriver on the Trent at Keadby in this photograph from around 1910; a group of barges has been turned by the steam tug that has brought them from Hull in order to stem the tide off the entrance to the S&SYN at Keadby. One of the barges has its mast in position, indicating that it will sail on the S&SYN, whilst the others will probably go up the navigation behind a horse.

TNC's steam tug *Little John* and three of their Trent size dumb barges lie in the newly constructed 190ft x 30ft Hazleford lock at its official opening in 1926. The building of locks after the First World War produced a deeper and more reliable depth of water in the river between Newark and Nottingham.

*Opposite above:* The TNC's towing barge *Barlock* or *Barlet*, having penned up the small Trent size Newark Town lock in 1934, waits to resume its tow of a dumb barge currently on passage through the lock. The lock remained a bottleneck for Trent traffic until it was replaced by a 190ft x 30ft structure in 1952.

*Opposite below:* A tow of Trent barges, handled by the TNC's steam tug *Little John*, heads up the Trent at Fiskerton above Newark in the 1920s. The tugmaster occasionally asked the barge captains to raise their sails when under tow and one vessel seems ready to do so here.

*Above:* Dumb craft that would have been towed up the Trent and probably horsed the short distance along the Nottingham Canal are shown in the 1920s outside this TNC depot at the city's Wilford Street.

*Below:* An Upper Trent vessel is partially shown in the 1900s near Trent lock at the entrance to the Erewash Canal where a waterway 'crossroads' is formed at the confluence of the rivers Soar and Trent. These shallow-drafted craft, with their characteristic cabin amidships, usually worked only above Newark, where cargoes were once transhipped into them from the Hull boats.

One of the small lighters, usually kept on the Fossdyke at Torksey for transhipping a barge's cargo into to lower the larger vessel's draft after it had left the Trent, is shown on Lincoln's Waterside which had been drained for maintenance. The vessel seems to be held in position by the bucket hoist from a nearby mill, whilst a chute is positioned to load a bagged cargo.

Holgates' 102½ft x 16½ft steel dumb barge, *Pat*, formerly *Leetham's Pat*, built by T.H. Scarr of Howdendyke in 1922. Formerly owned by Spillers and then Holgates, it can be seen here transhipping rye for Gainsborough from the coaster *Wotan* at Goole in 1986.

Waddingtons' *Progress* pulls their 75ft x 20ft, Dunston-built (in 1933) *No.40* past Sprotbrough wharf in 1999, laden with imported timber bound for Swinton. Pull tows were rare on the S&SYN above Doncaster and large vessels such as these were unable to reach this part of the navigation until the improvements of the 1980s. The earliest (18ft) width of Sprotbrough cut is illustrated on page 12; this was increased to 38ft in 1908, and to the width shown here in the improvements of the 1980s. (Mike Brown)

*Opposite above:* A one-off pull- (and push-) tow on the Trent in 1999 as the tug *Gillian Knight* and barge *Landrager 19* are photographed transporting a 300-ton transformer upriver near Torksey. The push-tug is obscured by the transformer.

*Opposite below:* Wynns' dumb, purpose-built, outsize load transporter, the 262ft x 54ft *Terra Marique*, carried its first cargo, a Concorde aeroplane, down the Thames en route to a museum in Scotland in April 2004. Built with the aid of a £8.5 million grant, the vessel was designed to transport Abnormal Indivisible Loads (AILs) by sea and on inland waterways. In the UK this may be done in conjunction with *Inland Navigator* described in *Tanker Barges on the Humber Waterways*, which can be carried inside the vessel. *Terra Marique* is shown under pull-tow by two of Acasters' tugs coming up the Trent below Gainsborough in May 2004, carrying a 270-ton transformer to Cottam power station. (John Noble collection)

# Ken Kettle, Calder Carrying Company Boatman

I started work with the Calder Carrying Company in 1937. In 1942, I was made captain of the wooden West Country size dumb boat *Salterhebble*, that had been built at Battye Ford in 1916 as *Thomas*. Its name had been changed in 1942 at the Admiralty's request to something more distinctive than *Thomas*.

My most memorable trip began after I had discharged coils of wire at Brighouse and was ordered to collect forty tons of coir from Alexandra Dock, Hull.

On the Calder and Hebble, I was supposed to use the company's horse, which was always otherwise engaged, or beg a tow from the captain of a passing motor barge. Towing fees were so low that it was hardly worthwhile for these captains to delay themselves by fastening me on and having two pennings at each lock, so I got to Wakefield by hitching short tows and bowhauling. It took a couple of days. Then Sugdens' power boat *David Sugden* pulled me to Goole. He didn't have a towing permit for the Ouse and Humber, so I had to book a tow to Hull with the Goole and Hull Steam Towing Company.

The next morning, I hung on to their tug *Salvage* in Ocean lock and we came out into the river at quite a lick. We hadn't gone more than a quarter of a mile before I realised that I couldn't steer. The rudder was completely out of the water, but the stem showed 5½ft. The tug crew were laughing so I just sat down to enjoy the run after I'd checked that the bilges were staying dry. After two and a half hours, instead of the usual four, we passed the mouth of the river Hull, the tug let go of my rope and I carried on smoothly to moor at the jetty outside Alexandra Dock and penned in later that day.

Sometimes I went up the river Hull to load cement at Earles and that involved moving stern first with the tide, dragging the anchor.

*Salterhebble* was fitted with a small Lister engine in 1944 and that made an enormous difference to my life aboard.

A West Country size keel is launched at Battye Ford yard on the C&HN near Mirfield, where Ken Kettle's *Salterhebble* was built.

three

Motorised Dumb Vessels

## George Trevethick, Marine Engineer

When my father brought his two diesel tugs here to Keadby in about 1930, several boatmen would never allow themselves to be towed by a diesel engine, only by a horse or steam tug. At the time there were several sailing craft running about with petrol/paraffin, semi-diesel or other experimental engines that had been fitted in the 1910s or 1920s, mainly as auxiliaries to help when they hadn't a fair wind. One vessel had a Jowett car engine standing on a strengthened head ledge shelf with a chain linked down to a shaft passing through the stern to drive a propellor; others had converted lorry engines fitted.

R.A. Lister & Co. of Dursley in Gloucestershire introduced their JP2 two-cylinder marine diesel engine in 1930 and this really caught on. During the 1930s every owner, whether of one vessel or a large fleet, then seemed to consider conversion of their dumb craft. Gardner, Ellwe, Petters, Widdop and Bolinder engines were also fitted, as well as Listers. JP stood for Joint Production, with Ruston & Hornsby of Lincoln, another company, like Listers, with origins in agricultural machinery. Following on from the 21hp JP2, Listers produced the 30hp three-cylinder JP3 and the 40hp four-cylinder JP4.

Almost all engines were fitted into the aft cabin, with the stern tube passing to the propellor through the shell of the vessel just to one side of its stern post. A few craft kept their aft cabin and had their engines placed in the hold, but this reduced carrying capacity.

Propellors with a diameter of between 2ft and 3½ft were fitted. The major manufacturers of these, and of stern gear, were Bruntons of Sudbury and Crowthers of Lancashire.

Such was the demand that boatyards in the area had waiting lists stretching into the 1940s for installations of engines into both wooden and steel vessels. Stanilands of Thorne, Waddingtons of Swinton, Warrens of New Holland and Woodwards of Beverley all specialised in this work; other yards fitted it in along with building new craft. The job usually took between two and three weeks. The Sheffield & South Yorkshire even supplied Lister JP2s on Hire Purchase to carriers on their navigation, such as Bleasdales, in the belief that they allowed faster working, more frequent cargo deliveries and, therefore, more income from tolls.

By 1941, the Ministry of Transport was offering loans for buying JP2s to carriers at only 3 per cent so that they could motorise their craft.

Several of the craft converted kept their tiller-steering and a weatherboard, but an equal number converted to wheel steering by having a wheel linked to the rudder using chains passing around radial quadrants. Then they had a wheelhouse fitted, though the old boatmen preferred canvas 'dodgers' because they didn't like navigating through glass.

I worked at Dunstons during the Second World War fitting steam engines into the TID tugs and 'puffers' they were building, but I was taken off this for two weeks in 1944 to fit a 60hp single-cylinder Widdop into Doncaster millers' keel *Danum*. The most important part of the job was lining things up. After I left Dunstons to form Keadby Marine, I fitted several engines including Lister JP4s to four of the six Sheffield size craft that Flixborough Shipping had had Dunstons build in the 1950s. Two were given engines when new but the company worked the four others as dumb barges for some time because they couldn't afford engines for them all at the time. I hired the dry dock at New Holland to do this over the years from 1956 to 1961. These were easier than most installations because the craft had been built for engines to be fitted. At that time, Listers cost about £11 per horsepower, so a JP4 would cost £440.

Many of the wheelboxes fitted to dumb craft looked like they were falling into the hold when the vessel was loaded. I tried to avoid this by building a full-size hardboard model of the wheelhouse. I put it in position on the barge, then moored it across the canal from me and shouted instructions to my assistant on board to adjust the level until it looked right.

A stern tube is shown fitted to one side of a steel vessel's stern post by Scarrs of Hessle when installing an engine in the 1920s.

The ketch-rigged 84ft x 20ft *Halcyon*, shown here, was built by Henry Scarr at Hessle in 1903 for Mark Aaron of Hull. An auxiliary engine by Plenty & Sons of Newbury was fitted in 1918 and Scarrs replaced this in 1922 with a Kromhout main engine. Described as a steel billyboy, the vessel voyaged on both inland waterways and seas, visiting most English East and South Coast ports, and occasionally crossing the North Sea.

Built by Joseph Scarr at Beverley in 1910 for Selby Oil Mills, the lighter *Leeds Magnetic* passed to Whitakers of Hull in 1956 after the oil mills opted to build a new fleet of SPVs. Whitakers immediately had a 6LW Gardner engine installed by their Yorkshire Dry Dock subsidiary and the 96½ft x 17½ft vessel is shown coming down a busy river Hull below Scott Street bridge shortly afterwards with its wheelhouse dismantled and steering chains visible.

*Opposite above:* T.F. Wood & Co. of York had the 90ft x 17ft *Bustardthorpe* built as a dumb barge by Watsons of Gainsborough in 1914, but opted to have it motorised in 1931. A 60hp Lister was fitted and replaced in 1966 by a 120hp Gardner. The vessel was never lengthened and is shown in 1989, when owned by Hornshaw Water Transport, on the A&CN at its junction with the New Junction Canal whilst returning light from Knottingley after delivering a load of Trent aggregate.

*Opposite below:* A small Petter engine was fitted to George Henry Holgate's 1923-built (by Scarrs of Hessle) keel *Radio* in 1937 and this was replaced by a Gardner engine in 1944. The 61½ft x 14½ft (slightly narrower than Sheffield size) vessel is shown in 1953, waiting to load coal for Hull or Beverley at Roundwood colliery staithe, on the S&SYN.

The Sheffield size sloop *Zenith*, later *Zenith A* and finally *Zenitha*, was built by Warrens of New Holland in 1925 for William Foster & Sons of Barton-on-Humber. An Ellwe engine was fitted in 1931 and the vessel was sold in 1946. It was lengthened to 76½ft and a 62hp Lister was fitted in 1957 after purchase by Eccles Transport and is shown in the Ouse off Goole with a dumb vessel fastened alongside when owned by Holgates in 1978. *Zenitha* subsequently reverted to a dumb barge.

*Above:* A 60hp Lister engine, wheel steering and wheelhouse were fitted to Nelson Blow's *Blow's Albert* (see pages 52–53) in 1951. The vessel was sold to Gilyott & Scott in 1977 and is shown here as *Albert* on the river Hull in 1983, with some of the alterations evident at the vessel's stern.

*Right:* The Calder Carrying Co.'s West Country size wooden dumb barge *Robert* was built at Mirfield in 1934, motorised by the installation in 1939 of a Lister JP2, and renamed *Cooper Bridge*. It is shown on the river Hull in the late 1940s, loading a return cargo for the C&HN. (*Hull Daily Mail*)

The Sheffield size *Otter* was built in 1899 by Warrens at Beverley for four joint-owners and sold to William Gilyott & Co., the Hull lighter owners, in 1909. After ownership had passed to Charles Walker of Thorne, a Lister JP2 was fitted in 1956 by Stanilands and the laden vessel is shown here in the 1960s entering Lofthouse Basin on the A&CN, near Stanley Ferry.

*Opposite above:* The motorised 65ft x 15½ft steel ex-sloop *Irby* (built as *Hope* at Beverley in 1897) is the most prominent of three craft frozen in at Burton Stather on the Trent in the early months of 1940. All three craft have masts to help handle bank-stoning material being carried at the time and a furled foresail is visible on one of them, indicating that this vessel had not yet been motorised.

*Opposite below: Misterton*, was built for Furley & Co. by Joseph Scarr at Beverley in 1923 to Lincoln size and motorised with a Lister JP2 in 1948. The vessel is shown heading up the S&SYN below Swinton lock in 1990 with coils of imported steel wire. Prior to 1980, before the Sheffield size locks had been replaced, *Misterton* was too long to use this part of the S&SYN above Doncaster.

*Northern King* was built in 1928 by Scarrs of Howdendyke as a 92ft x 18½ft dumb barge for Hudson Ward & Co., the millers. It was purchased by Waddingtons of Swinton in 1979; an air-cooled 138hp Lister had been fitted by them and the vessel is shown arriving at Knottingley, loaded with imported steel collected at Goole.

*Opposite above:* In 1905, the Sheffield size wooden keel *Guidance* was built for a member of the Schofield family by Worfolks of Stainforth. Fred Schofield had a 24hp Ailsa Craig engine installed in the mid-1930s before it was sold to a Goole company. The vessel was eventually purchased by Waddingtons of Swinton in 1950 after a 30hp Lister engine had been fitted, and used to carry coal on the S&SYN until it was sold for conversion to a Thames hotel boat. *Guidance* (nearer the camera) and *Laurel* are shown in 1973, moored at Keadby, prior to leaving for the voyage down the East Coast

*Opposite below:* In 1943 Mr and Mrs Eric Lister bowhauled the Manvers size steel dumb barge *Millgill*, built at Hessle as *Scaife's Olive* in 1897, from Thorne to Swinton after it had been bought by Waddingtons. A Lister JP2 was fitted, the vessel was renamed *Ethel* after Mrs Lister, and Eric was given captaincy of it. Making one of its regular deliveries of sand from Gunness to Redfearns' Barnsley glassworks, *Ethel* was the last vessel down the Barnsley Canal before the catastrophic burst of November 1946 and it is shown here shortly after that incident, on the S&SYN's Rotherham–Blackburn Meadows power station coal run.

The 75ft x 17ft dumb grain barge *Valour* was built in 1923 by T. Scarr at Howdendyke for William Holmes of Stainforth, who sold it to Leeds Industrial Co-operative Society in 1943. After purchase by Fred Moxon in 1956, the vessel was lengthened to 123ft and a 40hp McLaren engine installed. It is shown passing up the A&CN at Bulholme lock in the 1950s.

*Eleanor B* was built in 1924 for Jonas Braithwaite by Henry Scarr of Hessle. Its sole function was to collect coal for delivery to the river Hull wharf of Reckitts', the chemical company. A 40hp Atlantic engine was installed in 1946 after the vessel had been taken over by Reckitts themselves and *Eleanor B* is shown on the river Trent in the 1950s loaded with coal from Hatfield Colliery for its owners' premises.

*Above:* Earles' 68ft x 17½ft sloop *Miss Madeline* was built in 1925 by Warrens of New Holland and a 90hp Gardner engine fitted in 1951. The vessel, shown in the 1970s after being rebuilt and lengthened to 91ft by Harkers of Knottingley, is loading steel for export at Knostrop depot when owned by Gainsborough Shipping.

*Right:* James Barraclough & Co.'s steel sloop *Phyllis* (see page 21) was motorised in 1944 and is here shown viewed through the open window of a tanker barge's wheelhouse whilst coming down the A&CN at Whitley Bridge in the 1950s, probably with a return load of coal after delivering chalk to Thwaite Mills, near Leeds.

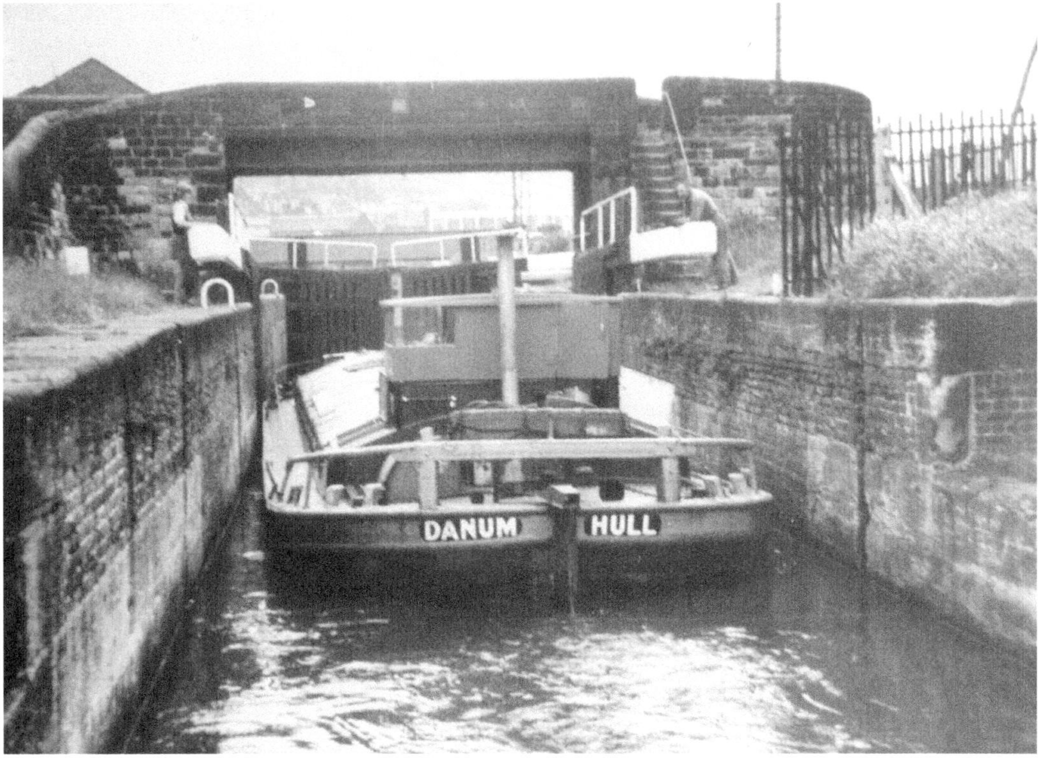
DANUM
HULL

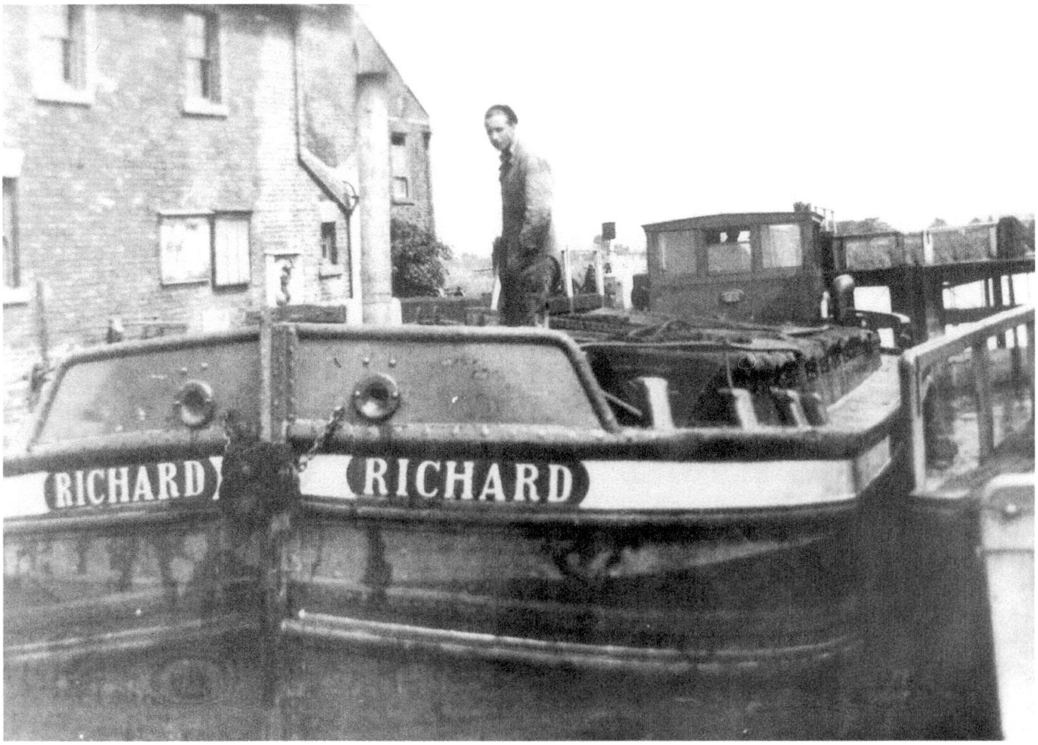
RICHARD
RICHARD

*Above:* John Hunt & Sons were founded in 1860 and brought many cargoes to Leeds, initially in dumb craft towed by the A&CN steam towing service and later by their own towing barge *Hunt's Brent*. *Hunt's Felix* was built dumb for Hunts in 1927 by Henry Scarr of Hessle and used for working along part of the L&LC to Watsons' soap factory on the river Aire above the weir at Leeds. It was motorised in 1950 with a 30hp Lister, following a policy change by the company in favour of SPVs and sold to Waddingtons of Swinton in 1964, after being shortened from its original 64ft to 61½ft. *Hunt's* was dropped from the vessel's name and it is shown entering the new lock at Sprotbrough in 1981 carrying one of the last loads of coal from Denaby for Doncaster power station. (John Noble collection)

*Opposite above:* The keel *Danum* (shown being bowhauled on page 36) was built in 1932 by Dunstons at Thorne for the small fleet of Thomas Hanley & Sons, the Doncaster millers. It was motorised by Dunstons in 1944 (see page 66), passed to Ranks when Hanleys was taken over, and is shown entering Rotherham lock in the 1960s, bound for the Hovis mill on the river Rother.

*Opposite below:* Richard Hodgson & Sons, the Beverley tanners, began to build up a fleet of barges with secondhand craft and the 1940 Dunston of Thorne, Sheffield size newbuilding, *Richard*. The vessel was worked dumb until 1943 when a Lister JP3 was installed and is shown later in the 1940s leaving Keadby lock to enter the S&SYN and collect a cargo of coal from Hatfield for its owners. (Les Hill)

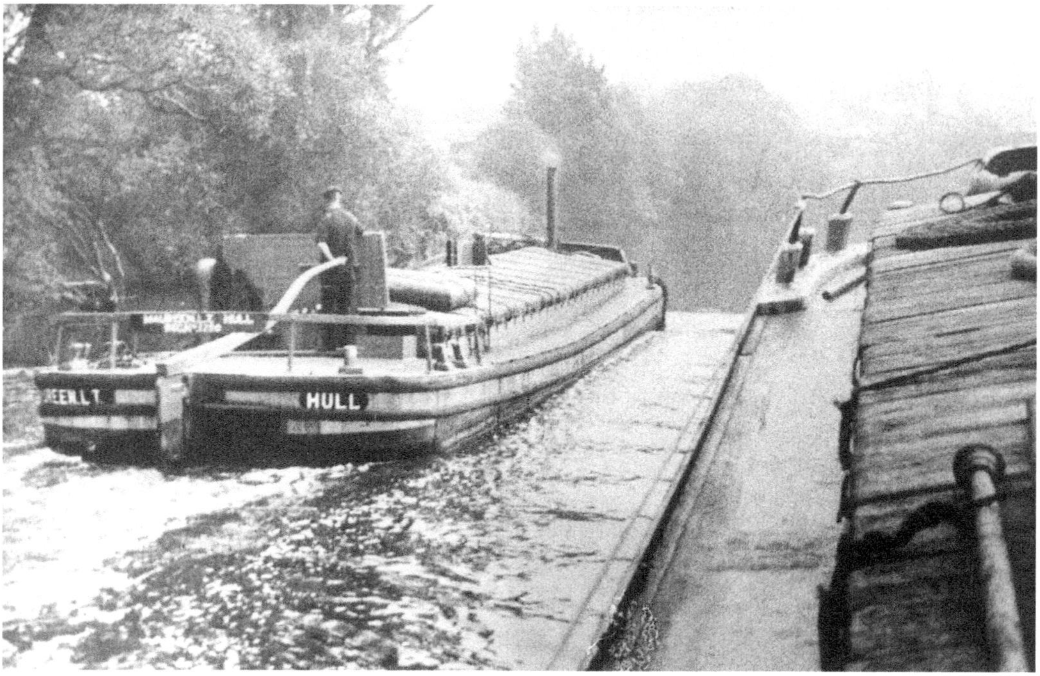
HULL

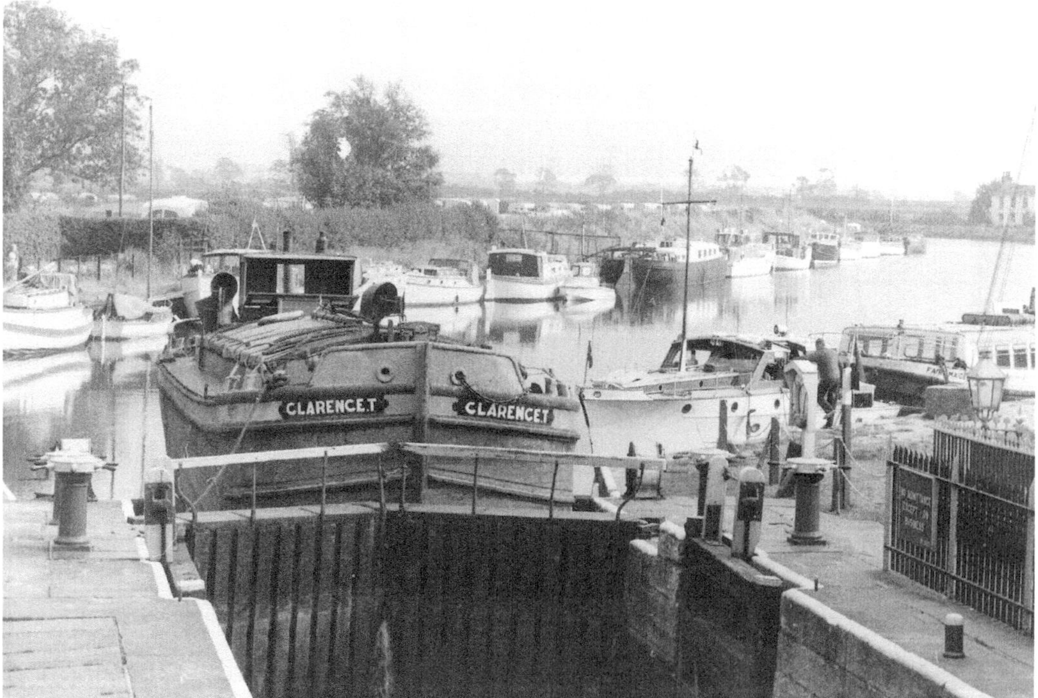
CLARENCE.T
CLARENCE.T

Seven Sheffield size keels were built for the S&SYNC in 1925 by Dunstons, four of which were sold under Hire Purchase agreements to W. Bleasdale & Co. of Hull, one of the major carriers on the S&SYN. *Attercliffe* was one of these. In 1936 Bleasdales also purchased six 21hp Lister engines from the S&SYNC under other HP agreements and *Attercliffe* received one of these in 1937. The motorised vessel is shown, during the Second World War, in Sheffield basin with the Straddle warehouse (built 1896–1898 and not present on the picture on page 36) prominent.

*Opposite above:* 'John Joe' Tomlinson built up a fleet consisting mainly of sloops, named with the suffix *T*. *Maureen L T* was built as the Sheffield size keel *Peggy Birch* in 1907 by Joseph Scarr of Beverley, renamed *Peggy T* in 1929 and motorised with a Lister JP2 in 1948. The vessel is shown heading up the river section of the S&SYN above Doncaster in the 1950s with a cargo loaded at Hull.

*Opposite below:* J.J. Tomlinson's *Clarence T*, pictured as a sloop on page 24, had a Lister JP4 installed in 1956. The vessel is shown returning light from Lincoln to Hull waiting to pen through Torksey lock into the river Trent in 1962. (Norman Burnitt)

Furley & Co.'s Lincoln size dumb barge *Lindum* was built in 1923 by Joseph Scarr & Son of Beverley and a Lister JP3 was installed during 1950. The vessel is shown loaded in 1951 as it tows a lighter down the river Witham from Brayford towards Lincoln's 'Glory Hole'. (John Noble collection)

*Opposite above:* In 1937 Bleasdales' Sheffield size *Lightcliffe*, built in 1924 by Dunstons of Thorne, also received one of the 21hp Lister engines purchased from the S&SYNC. The vessel is shown discharging boxes of ferrosilicon in the southern corner of the Sheffield basin in the 1960s after being seized from Bleasdales by the BTC in 1958 for non-payment of tolls. Both Attercliffe and Lightcliffe can be seen to have retained their tiller steering which left the helmsman exposed to the elements.

*Opposite below: Loxley* was another of the seven keels built for the S&SYNC by Dunstons in 1925 and one of the three sold under a Hire Purchase agreement to Furleys. Unlike *Attercliffe*, *Loxley* was not motorised until a Lister JP3 was installed in 1953 and it was sold to Waddingtons in 1965. It is shown here under repair at Hepworths of Paull in the late 1950s following a collision in the Humber.

Another ex-AC (ammunition carrying) barge, built before the First World War, was *Dumbuck*, discovered by Wilf Acaster in 1956 lying in Scotland where Loch Lomond runs into the Clyde and brought to the Humber as a dumb barge. An 88hp Kelvin engine was fitted by Warrens in the mid-1950s and the vessel joined Acasters' small fleet. The engine was replaced by a 112hp Kelvin in 1970 and *Dumbuck* is shown here, with a dumb barge fastened alongside, on the S&SYN at Long Sandall in 1980.

*Opposite above:* Warrens of New Holland built the Lincoln size *Brayford* in 1925 for Lincoln & Hull Water Transport Co and the vessel carried 80-ton cargoes of grain from Hull to Lincoln's Co-op Mill for many years. The vessel was motorised in 1946 and is shown outside the mill in the late 1960s. Deliveries to the mill by water ended in 1971. (Mike Black)

*Opposite below:* As well as deliveries of grain, Lincoln & Hull were extensively involved in the carriage of Trent aggregate, for which purpose they bought several dumb 220-ton capacity, 126ft x 16½ft AC steel barges, built for service in the First World War. *AC 2* was one of these which was motorised by the company in the 1950s when a 110hp Gardner was fitted. It is shown here (left) after finishing work on the gravel trade in 1967, being used on salvage work, a rapidly developing activity of the company, in Grimsby Docks.

Built as the dumb barge *I.W.N.E. No.2* by Harkers in 1949 for the D&IWE, the BTC decided to move away from pull towing and this vessel plus its sister ship, *No.1* (see page 44), were lengthened in the mid-1950s to 90ft x 15½ft. 54 Lister Freedom engines were also installed. *No.1* was renamed *Delta BW* and *No.2*, shown here transhipping coils of wire at Hull, *Lambda BW*. (Associated British Ports)

*Opposite above:* The Flixborough Shipping Co ordered six Sheffield size steel craft from Dunstons of Thorne and these were built in 1953. A four-and-a-half-year wait for delivery of engines led to four of the craft being worked as dumb barges for a time. *Littlebeck* was one of these, but was fitted with a Lister JP4 by George Trevethick's Keadby Marine in 1961 and is shown passing Harkers' yard at Knottingley in 1968, shortly after its owners' newest vessel, *Risby*, had been launched, loaded with coal from Parkhill colliery for Flixborough wharf on the river Trent.

*Below:* The 70ft x 19ft dumb lighter *P.O.E.M. 22* was built by Dunstons of Thorne in 1956 for Hull's Premier Oil Extraction Mills. It was sold to Gilyott & Scott in 1968 and the outboard-type Harbormaster-66 propulsion unit, with its wheel at right angles to the usual position, was fitted in the mid-1970s. It is shown coming light down the river Hull above Drypool Bridge in 1979.

Hargreaves' 80ft x 16½ft *No.5*, was built dumb by Dunstons of Thorne in 1958 but fitted to receive an engine if and when the company changed over from tug-hauled dumb craft to SPVs. This duly happened and, after being worked as a dumb barge for some years, a Lister JP4 was fitted to *No.5* in the mid-1960s and the vessel is shown in 1983 heading down the 'five-mile pond' of the river Aire below Castleford, loaded with coal from Fryston colliery for Ferrybridge 'B' power station.

*Opposite above:* Hargreaves motorised both 80ft x 16½ft dumb barges *Joyce* (left) and *Ann* in the early 1960s at their Castleford Dockyard with 48hp engines and fitted wheel steering. They did this to all fifteen of their Ferrybridge 'B' barges. In the 1980s, however, they chose to remove the engines from some of the craft and fit more powerful units to others. *Joyce* was made dumb whilst *Ann* received a 100hp Kelvin engine enabling it to tow a dumb barge. The pair are shown swinging in Savile staithe on the A&CN in 1985, shortly before it closed, with *Ann* neither pull- nor push-towing.

*Right:* Built for Bleasdales in 1922 by Watsons of Gainsborough as a 71½ft x 17ft dumb barge, *Heathercliffe*, like *Lightcliffe* on pages 82–83, was taken over by the BTC for non-payment of tolls. In 1960, it was purchased by G.D. Holmes of Goole, renamed *Valiant H*, lengthened to 106½ft and fitted with a 150hp Gardner by Harkers in 1962. Next, it was sold to James Barraclough & Co. in 1972 and is shown here in 1982 discharging a cargo at Trent Lane, Nottingham, with another ex-Barraclough vessel, *Juneville*, moored alongside. Both craft were owned by Gainsborough Shipping at the time, having been purchased in 1975. (John Noble collection)

Robinsons' Dunstons-built (c.1900) wooden keel *Annie Maud* was shown on page 40 being hauled by horse. It was purchased by Waddingtons of Swinton in 1937 and had a 21hp Lister JP2 fitted. In 1974 it was sold to Castle Mills Museum at York for preservation, but wooden craft are notoriously expensive, time-consuming and difficult to maintain in a preserved state. Consequently it was decided to scrap *Annie Maud* and the vessel is seen partly broken up on the Foss riverbank outside the museum in 1979. (Malcolm Slater)

four

Built as SPVs

During the 1930s there was a smooth transition at boatyards from building dumb craft to producing new self-propelled vessels (SPVs). This occurred during a marked decline in the demand for wooden boats, though production of motorised wooden craft survived at Mirfield until 1955. By the end of the 1930s the builders of steel craft were prospering, though sizes of most vessels were still limited by dimensions of the navigations on which they were expected to trade, such as the S&SYN, Trent and Fossdyke.

By the 1950s steel specialists established in the late nineteenth century, such as Dunstons of Thorne, Henry Scarr of Hessle (taken over by Dunstons in 1931 but not assuming their name until the 1950s), Joseph Scarr & Sons of Beverley, Watsons of Gainsborough (actually Beckingham) and Warrens of New Holland, had been joined by Harkers of Knottingley, Hepworths of Paull, Scarrs (initially T.H., subsequently D.E.) of Howdendyke and the Yorkshire Dry Dock Co. of Hull. A few other companies, such as Camplings of Goole, Waddingtons of Swinton and Cooks of New Holland (on the former site of Warrens), also tried their hands at boatbuilding in steel. Two other yards, Cochranes of Selby and Cook, Welton & Gemmell of Beverley, who both specialised in sea-going vessels, also built a few inland waterway craft.

In the 1930s boatmen had considered that a 21hp engine was more than adequate to power a vessel that could readily be moved by 1hp but, by the early 1970s, larger vessels were being built and 375hp engines had been fitted to a few craft.

A few sea-going vessels, most built at Humber yards, have also been included in this chapter. The examples chosen worked regularly to ports on the inland waterways of the Humber.

This chapter also contains, on page 112, an operator's account of problems encountered in the 1990s when he felt that BWB was failing to honour an agreement made with the EU over the improved S&SYN and was using their funds unwisely to facilitate usage of the waterways by pleasure craft.

*Opposite:* One of the first motor vessels to be built in the region was produced at Hunters' yard on Beverley Beck in 1921. The 77ft x 17ft wooden *Hall's Avance*, shown on the stocks waiting to be launched, was built as a sloop but powered by a semi-diesel Swedish engine. This was a rare new vessel to be added to Fred Hall's fleet of reconditioned craft and worked out of the Humber to the Wash ports, as well as up to Leeds. Fred Hall's 'yacht' is moored in the foreground. *Hall's Avance* was lost in 1941 whilst on Admiralty service. (D. Grindell collection)

*Above:* Possibly the earliest photograph of one of the first SPVs on the Humber waterways, this shows the 59½ft x 14½ft *Reklaw* moored on the river Foss in the late 1920s outside the Layerthorpe yard of its York owners, J.H. Walker & Co. The vessel, fitted with a 50bhp Kromhout engine, was built by T.H. Scarr of Howdendyke in 1925 and used to win building sand, handled using the mast and derrick, from the Ouse and nearby rivers for over half a century. (Ron Cowl collection)

*Right: Reklaw* was still at work around York in the late 1970s after a wheelhouse had been fitted and the mast and derrick replaced by a crane and grab, thus reducing its capacity from 100 tons to about 65 tons. The vessel is shown setting out to collect another cargo on an icy river Ouse in 1975. (Ron Cowl)

Dunstons built the 76½ft x 17ft SPV *A Victory* for James Barraclough & Co. in 1929. The vessel, fitted with a 90hp Ellwe engine, is shown discharging chalk at Thwaite Mills, on the A&CN, near Leeds, in the 1940s. Though never a sailing vessel, *A Victory* was fitted with a mast which, in conjunction with a derrick, was often eseential in loading and discharging its cargoes. (A. Horn collection)

The first dry cargo motor barge to be built by Harkers was the 75ft x 14½ft *Stedfast*, completed in 1932 for James Wilby, the West Yorkshire coal carrier. The vessel is shown crossing the A&CN's Stanley Ferry aqueduct in 1958. (BWB)

John Hunt & Sons had their 76½ft x 15½ft motor barge *Henry Hunt* built in 1934 by Henry Scarr at Hessle and fitted with a Lister JP4 engine. It is shown loading a cargo, almost certainly bound for Leeds, overside from a Finnish ship in Hull's Alexandra Dock in 1962, after being re-engined in 1961 with a 78hp Petter. (Associated British Ports)

*Above:* Built in 1934 by Woodwards on the river Hull site of the former Joseph Scarr yard at Grovehill, Beverley, James Barraclough & Co.'s 200-ton capacity, 80ft x 17ft motor barge *Maranne* is shown discharging grain at King's Mill, Knottingley, in the early 1960s.

*Left:* The Sheffield size motor barge *Lys* was built at Hessle in 1937 by Henry Scarr for Furley & Co. It was sold in 1965 to Hubert Barrass and is shown on the S&YSYN in the early 1970s under his ownership, shortly after leaving Aldwarke lock, bound for Rotherham's Hovis mill.

*Right:* Furleys' Dunstons-built – in 1938 – Sheffield size *Riccall* was fitted with a 40hp Ellwe engine when new and is shown, after its 1965 sale to Waddingtons, discharging coal from Denaby at Doncaster power station.

*Below:* The first SPV owned by James Hargreaves & Sons of Leeds was built by Harkers in 1938 and was the steel West Country size *No.61*, fitted with an Ellwe engine and shown here on the C&HN in 1979 as it left the upper Figure of Three locks.

The 124ft x 17½ft *Eskdale H* was built by Harkers in 1946 and added to their tanker fleet. In 1968 it was converted, like many other tankers that were over fifteen years old, less sophisticated and smaller than those being built at the time, into a dry cargo barge and bought by John Branford who used it mainly to deliver Trent aggregate to Knottingley. The vessel is shown at Keadby loading sand brought from the quarry by lorry. The barge began life with a Gardner engine which was replaced by a Lister-Blackstone and, at the time of the photograph, another Gardner had been installed.

Richard Hodgson & Sons, the tanners of Beverley, had several Sheffield size *-tans* built in 1950 by Hepworths at Paull. Their *Sectan*, and *Richard* (see page 78–79) are shown ice-bound on the river Hull below Beverley in early 1963.

The BTC's 72½ft x 15½ft motor barge *Kappa BW*, built as an SPV by Dunstons in 1954, and *Delta BW*, the now 90ft x 15½ft lengthened and motorised former *I.W.N.E. No.1* (shown on page 44), loading overside from *Carlo* in Hull's Alexandra Dock in the late 1950s. Both were fitted with 54hp Lister Freedom engines at the time. *Kappa* was later lengthened to 106ft. (BWB)

Few wooden SPVs were built on the Humber waterways but Ledgard Bridge Boatyard continued to produce motorised West Country size craft until 1955. This Hargreaves subsidiary's next-to-last new build was *BraDsyldA*, fitted with a Lister JP2, for the Bradford Dyers Association. It is shown being launched in 1954.

Waddingtons had the two Sheffield size SPVs *Onward* and *Forward* built at Harkers in 1954. They were both brought to Swinton to be fitted out and have Lister JP3 engines installed. *Forward* is shown on the 'top level' of the S&SYN as it approaches Sheffield with a cargo of wheat from Hull in 1958. (Reg Frost/Mrs C. Bird collection)

The lengthening in 1964 of the 104ft x 17½ft *Keewhit* to 126ft is shown. Built for Whitakers in 1955 by YDDC, both it and sister vessel *Sirwin* were converted to tanker barges in the 1970s when their owner decided to concentrate on carriage of liquid cargoes.

*Above:* Designed and built by Camplings of Goole in 1956 as a Sheffield size vessel for Rafferty & Watson, the Hull coal merchants, *Kirkby* is shown on York's river Foss carrying paper imported via Goole to the local newspaper's printing office in 1990. The vessel was first lengthened and refurbished at Camplings in the 1960s, then shortened to 85½ft in the 1980s to allow it to pass through the Foss's Castle Mills lock. (Mike Brown)

The former *Gladys Lillian*, 111ft x 17½ft when built in 1957 by Dunstons for the BTC, is shown light at Carlton wharf on the Trent in 2006, prior to going down to Besthorpe staithe to load aggregate for Whitwood on the A&CN. This was the vessel's first trip following lengthening by a further 16ft (it had previously been stretched to 140ft), fitting of *Brocodale*'s bows (evident on this view) and renaming *Heather Rose H*, after the daughter of its present owner, Kevin Hornshaw. (John Noble)

*Opposite below:* Until the early 1950s, Associated Humber Lines (AHL) initially owned and then subsequently managed steam ships which traded across the North Sea from Humber ports, chiefly Goole. One of AHL's first diesel-powered, managed ships was the BTC's *Byland Abbey*, built at Sunderland in 1956 and registered at Goole. The ship, shown on this AHL publicity card, joined the company's Goole-Copenhagen 'butter boat' service in 1957, regularly passing over the 60 miles of Humber waterway between Spurn and Goole. (Brian Masterman collection)

*Above:* The Lincoln size SPV *Tess* was built in 1959 by Hepworths for Furley & Co. and is shown immediately after its launch into the Humber at Paull. (John Noble collection)

*Below:* The final Sheffield size dry cargo vessel to be built, *Heritage*, was constructed at Waddingtons' Swinton yard and launched in 1960. It is seen here in 1979 on the Denaby-Doncaster power station coal trade, viewed from the top of Conisbrough viaduct.

*Above: Sirwin* (104ft x 17½ft, YDDC-built in 1955, lengthened to 127ft in 1963) beneath the chute at the old Besthorpe jetty on the Trent, waiting to load aggregate, with *Humber Trader* (125½ft x 17½ft, YDDC-built in 1958, never lengthened) at the extreme left of the picture and *Humber Navigator* (124ft x 19½ft, YDDC-built in 1964) in 1966. All craft were owned by Whitakers. (John Noble collection)

*Below:* Loaded SPVs including Les Hill's *Misterton* (see pages 72–73), Furleys' *Soar* (Lincoln size, built Hepworths 1959) and Flixborough Shipping's *Olga R* (Lincoln size, built Hepworths 1960), in the entrance lock to Hull's King George Dock preparing to pen out into the Humber in the mid-1960s and catch the 'first of flood' to begin their voyages.

Fitted into Dunstons' building programme before the BOCM Selby fleet was completed, Cawoods Wharton had fourteen new 83ft x 17ft, 200-ton capacity SPVs built between November 1961 and April 1962 to service the new Skelton Grange power station, near Leeds. They were powered by uprated Lister JP4 engines, developing 62hp and coal was collected from nearby staithes on the A&CN, mainly Savile and Astley. *No.7* is seen beneath the chute after loading at Water Haigh staithe. (Jarvis Whitton)

*Opposite above:* After Selby oil mills became part of BOCM in 1951, it was decided to replace their fleet of tugs and dumb barges that were then in use, with 97ft x 17½ft SPVs and eighteen of these 200-ton capacity barges were built by Dunstons between 1952 and 1963. *Selby Corrie*, one of the first to be built, is shown with other loaded inland waterway craft leaving the entrance lock to Hull's King George Dock in the mid-1960s at the start of its early-morning voyage to Selby.

*Opposite below:* The first floating elevator at Hull was installed in 1955. Selby barges, both the new SPVs and old dumb vessels are shown loading seeds from a ship in 1963 via three floating elevators moored alongside in King George Dock. (Associated British Ports)

The 125ft x 17½ft *Nora Easting* was built in 1964 by Harkers for the Flixborough Shipping Co. and is shown coming up the Trent light in the late 1960s, just above Gainsborough Bridge. The vessel had a new life under the name *Chaceley* when it moved to the river Severn in the mid-1970s. (John Noble collection)

The 137ft x 21½ft graveller *Normanton*, powered by a 150hp Gardner, was built for Lincoln & Hull Water Transport Co. by Harkers in 1967. It is shown in Grimsby Docks delivering a cargo of Trent aggregate in the 1970s. (John Noble collection)

The 145ft x 23ft *Havitgood I*, built by Hepworths in 1968 as a coal barge for Good, Havercroft & Co., was sold in 1975 to Steetleys. It shipped water whilst coming downriver fully loaded in 1983 and is seen beached on Hessle foreshore in the shade of the Humber Bridge. The vessel was salvaged and then purchased by Lincoln & Hull Marine Contractors who renamed it *Torksey*. (John Noble collection)

PHOENIX

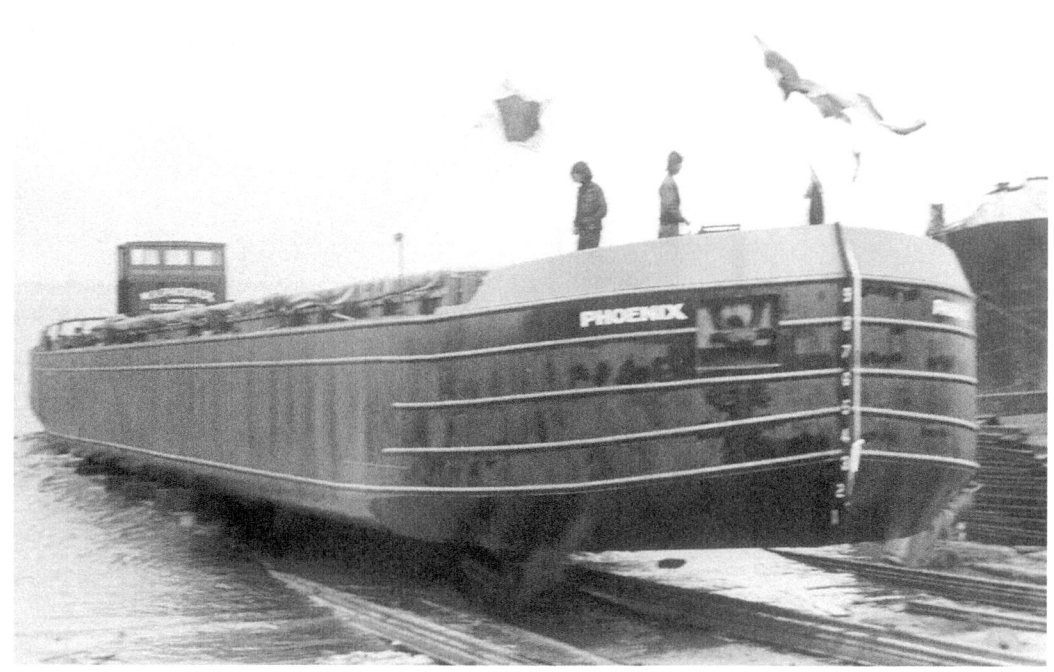

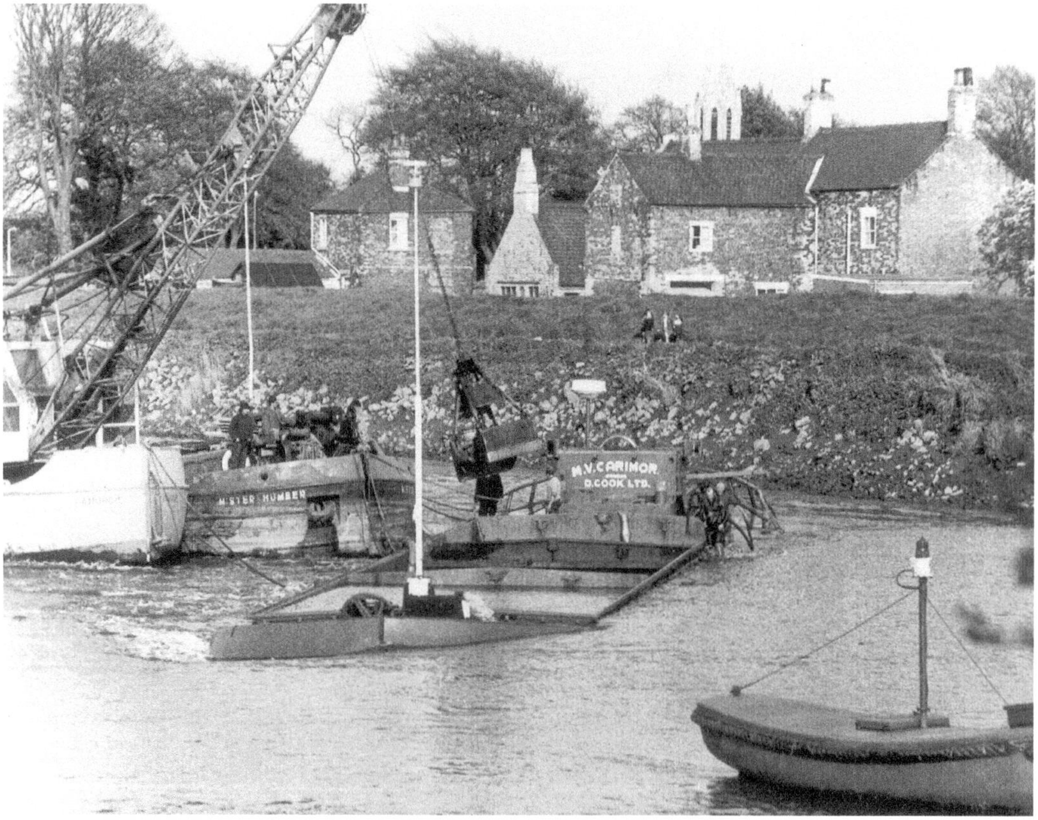
M.V.CARIMOR
D.COOK LTD.

At 150ft x 28ft and powered by a 375hp Kelvin engine, Lincoln & Hull's *Collingham*, built by YDDC in 1974, was the joint largest barge to work on the Humber waterways (*Swinderby*, their other giant was built in the same year at New Holland Shipyard). *Collingham* is shown on its maiden voyage during loading at Girton quarry staithe. When tides and water levels were right, they could each carry 750 tons of Trent gravel. (John Noble collection)

*Opposite above and below:* Built at D. Cook's New Holland Shipyard in 1972, for his aggregate-carrying operation, the 149ft x 20ft *Phoenix* obviously caught out the photographer when it was launched. The vessel was almost immediately renamed *Carimor*. The photograph (below) was taken in 1975 on the Trent between East and West Stockwith after it had run aground fully loaded, holing the engine cabin on rocks. In 1979 *Carimor* sank again in the Humber. (John Noble collection)

> Extracts from notes by Victor Waddington based on the captain's report of a voyage from Goole to Eastwood on 10 December 1995 aboard *Progress,* loaded to a draught of 7ft 10ins, which were forwarded to BWB. Edited with summaries in italics by Mike Taylor
>
> Entering the New Junction Canal we slid through a large hill of mud for a couple of lengths. The barge sheered off course and one could imagine why BWB state that our men cannot steer a straight course. The same could be said of the length between Sykehouse Road Bridge and the next bridge. Needs deepening for craft of today's draught, beam and length. The published draught claims to be 2.4m (8ft 3ins)
>
> We were forced to stop below Kirkhouse Green Swing Bridge until the bridge was raised and were aground approximately 50ft from the bridge. Coming to Goole last week, we had to wait for half an hour for the bridge to be opened, there were pleasure craft tied up at the nearby moorings and we were blown almost into them. BWB do not understand that a long vessel, ballasted down at the stern to keep the prop under water, will have its bows almost out of water catching every breath of wind. There is no problem if it can keep moving, but if not, safety is put at risk.
>
> *BWB-built pleasure craft facilities at Barnby Dun and Long Sandall lock were then described as being sited with no consideration for large commercial craft.*
>
> Below Doncaster lock is the most dangerous place on the navigation. Pleasure craft are tied up near the lock entrance waiting to use the rubbish disposal, toilet facilities or water point in an area that is in urgent need of dredging. The thick black mud we stir up clogs our cooling system filters, we have to push through the mud hill trying to keep to our course and, at the same time, slow down to enter the lock. BW seem not to understand about barges pushing through mud close to bridges and locks and sheering off course. BW Management and Staff does not contain one single boatman!
>
> The river is teeming with fish, fishermen are digging themselves places in the banks and in many places building stages to sit and fish from. They expect craft to ease down so as not to wash their tackle away. If we comply vessels can lose steerage and go anywhere, if we don't, we are subjected to abuse and even missiles.
>
> *The report continues in similar vein to the end of the voyage, with "sludge preventing the vessel responding" at Mexborough Double Bridges and Kilnhurst Railway Bridge and "damaging blows from a hard underwater object" at several points between Mexborough and Eastwood.*
>
> BWB nowadays seem to concentrate on the appearance of the waterway ABOVE WATER. The grass is cut regularly and lock gates are kept well painted, unfortunately by redundant dredger crews. The situation BENEATH the water is totally ignored and obstacles stay there however often they are reported.

In the 1990s, Victor Waddington, then with over seventy years' experience of carrying cargoes on the S&SYN, conducted a campaign against the unsatisfactory, unpublicised state of 'his' waterway which, after its £16 million improvements, completed in 1983, had been allowed to deteriorate due to a lack of dredging (the dredgers had been sold) and under-manning (mobile lock and bridge keepers in vans had taken the places of resident staff, leading to delays). Furthermore, he felt that facilities for pleasure craft had been provided with little regard for the safety of their occupants.

Representative of several short sea coasters that were built on the Humber waterways and subsequently became regular traders on them, *Alice P.G.* was built for Giles W. Pritchard Gordon in 1978. The ship is shown rounding Morton Corner on the Trent in 1983, after delivering a cargo to Gainsborough.

Another sea-going vessel built on the Humber waterways which became a frequent visitor to them was *Willonia*, launched at Cochranes' Shipyard, Selby, in 1984 and shown there on the Ouse being fitted out. This ship was also owned by a local company, J. Wharton (Shipping), based on the river Trent at Gunness, and used to deliver cargoes from mainland Europe to their wharves.

Union Transport (UT) have been regular traders at the Humber ports and Trent wharves since the company began shipowning in 1973. Some of their ships have been built locally by Cochranes of Selby and the YDDC of Hull. Here, their *Union Mercury* is waiting to be launched at Selby in 1990 with the tugs *Riverman* and *Keelman* in attendance. Sadly, this particular ship made no voyages for UT because they refused to accept it after a sister ship had experienced serious problems with its hatch covers. After being laid up for a few months, it was sold and renamed *Betty-Jean C*.

five

# Push-Towed Craft

The two great advantages of push-towing over pull-towing are that only the tug needs to be manned when the tow is moving and the barges, chained tightly together to form a rigid unit when being push-towed, are more easily controlled than when they are roped together in a line behind the tug in pull-towing.

Cawoods Hargreaves were the first company on the Humber waterways to commit themselves to push-towed craft in the early 1960s. They had Dunstons build them a fleet of nine tugs and thirty-five 55½ft x 17ft dumb barges (pans) with a depth of 9½ft for coal deliveries to Ferrybridge 'C' power station. Shortly afterwards BWB entered the scene and they were followed by BACAT in the early 1970s using rectangular-section dumb barges that were slightly less than Sheffield size. Since then, private operators such as Waddingtons, Acasters and Branfords have also embraced the idea and pushed a whole variety of old lighters and dumbed down craft. In more recent times, Dean's Tugs have reintroduced the 61½ft x 31ft LASH barges on the Humber waterways.

As in Chapter Two, the tugs themselves have already been dealt with in *Tugs and Towing Barges on the Humber Waterways*. The final two chapters of that book cover push-towing, and here the actual cargo-carrying craft are featured.

Cawoods Hargreaves' *CH 106* starting to push three pans, loaded at Kellingley colliery, out of Ferrybridge flood lock in 1985.

A loaded pan being lifted for discharge at the Ferrybridge 'C' power station hoist in the 1980s.

## Douglas Carey, Cawoods Hargreaves' tug skipper

I started with Hargreaves in 1948 and moved to Cawoods Hargreaves in 1974. They had begun delivering coal to Ferrybridge 'C' station in 1967 and eventually had nine tugs and thirty-five compartment boats, all built by Dunstons at Thorne especially for the job.

The pans were usually loaded at colliery basins and staithes, where opencast coal, coal from collieries not on the water, and later imported coal was lorried to. All these were in an approximately 15-mile radius of the power station. The pans were worked in trains of three and these, plus a tug, were fastened rigidly together making a unit 195ft long, carrying over 500 tons when loaded. Loaded pans had a draught of 8ft and were pushed, but light pans were usually pulled due to the difficulty the helmsman would have looking over light pans high in the water if the tug was pushing.

The original plan was to have TWO hoists at the power station, but early economies left only one being built. When it was working, it was very impressive; quiet and efficent, lifting a loaded pan, tipping it and lowering it back into the water within ten minutes. When it broke down, though, there was always a delay and the time taken to get it back to working order ranged from a few days to over a year. The power station owners knew what they were doing when they planned for coal to come by both rail and water. Rail always made the bigger deliveries and also benefitted when the hoist was out of action. When working, we averaged fourteen pan sets a day, some days we managed seventeen or eighteen. In the first twenty years, four pan sets a day usually came from Fryston and four from Astley.

Despite the hoist, the miners' strikes of 1974 and 1984, the closure of feeder basins in the 1980s as their collieries became worked out, and the flooding of the major opencast site in 1988, the traffic continued until well after I'd retired in 1990. When it did finish in 2002, over 43 million tons of coal had been delivered to the power station in the thirty-five years since the traffic began.

*Above:* Prior to becomimg involved in the BACAT operation, BWB had embarked on push towing and were replacing their general cargo craft with 55ft x 15½ft HS (Humber Small) barges. One is seen loading from *City of Liverpool* in King George Dock, Hull, in 1970. (Associated British Ports)

*Left: Freight Trader* pushes three HS pans up the S&SYN past the old depot at Rotherham in 1973. (Norman Burnitt)

*Right:* The passage of a three-pan train of HS pans and their tug passing through the S&SYN's locks above Doncaster involved four pennings at each one and took up to an hour. Unsafe practices abounded here at Aldwarke lock where one slip by the human horse could have him trapped between a moving barge and the lock wall.

*Below:* BACAT barges are being placed on the deck of the mother ship at Hull's Riverside Quay in 1974 as the system began operating. YDDC built sixty-three of these 55ft x 15½ft craft, very similar to the nine HS pans they had built for BWB. (BWB)

BACAT pans purchased by BWB are shown at the official opening of the new lock at Sprotbrough in 1981 as the S&SYN improvement scheme was underway. (BWB)

*Opposite above:* A two-barge BACAT tow on the A&CN, en route from Leeds to Hull, passes Ferrybridge 'A' power station in 1974. (BWB)

*Opposite below:* Contrasting markedly with publicity for the system, this 'dog's hind leg' formation of a Rotherham-bound tow of loaded BACAT barges was photographed on the S&SYN after its time-consuming passage through the Sheffield size Aldwarke lock.

As mentioned on pages 88–89, some of Hargreaves' motorised, 200-ton capacity, former dumb barges had their engines replaced by 100hp engines in the early 1980s, whilst others had their engines removed and were push towed as dumb barges. *Santa Maria*, shown here loading at Astley staithe, was one of the latter.

*Opposite above:* A Hargreaves' motor/dumb barge pair approaching Ferrybridge 'B' power station in 1982 loaded with a total of over 400 tons of coal. (BWB)

*Opposite below:* The first push-tugs to be built in the UK were the 'Bantams', introduced in 1951. They found a variety of work on inland waterways and flooded quarries. Bantam tug *No.28* is shown, still at work in 1994, pushing a loaded aggregate barge downriver on the river Soar Navigation, near Leicester.

61½ft x 31ft LASH barges first appeared on the Humber in 1974 when the BACAT mother ship transported a few of them. They worked between Hull and either Selby or Beckingham and one of BWB's former Port of London Authority push tugs is shown handling two of them off Hull's Riverside Quay at the time. (BWB)

After the demise of the BACAT operation, which lasted for only eighteen months, LASH vanished from the Humber scene until late 1997 when John Dean's tugs began to handle them. Here a pair of the barges, loaded with rice for Selby is being pushed up the Ouse at Boothferry in 2001.

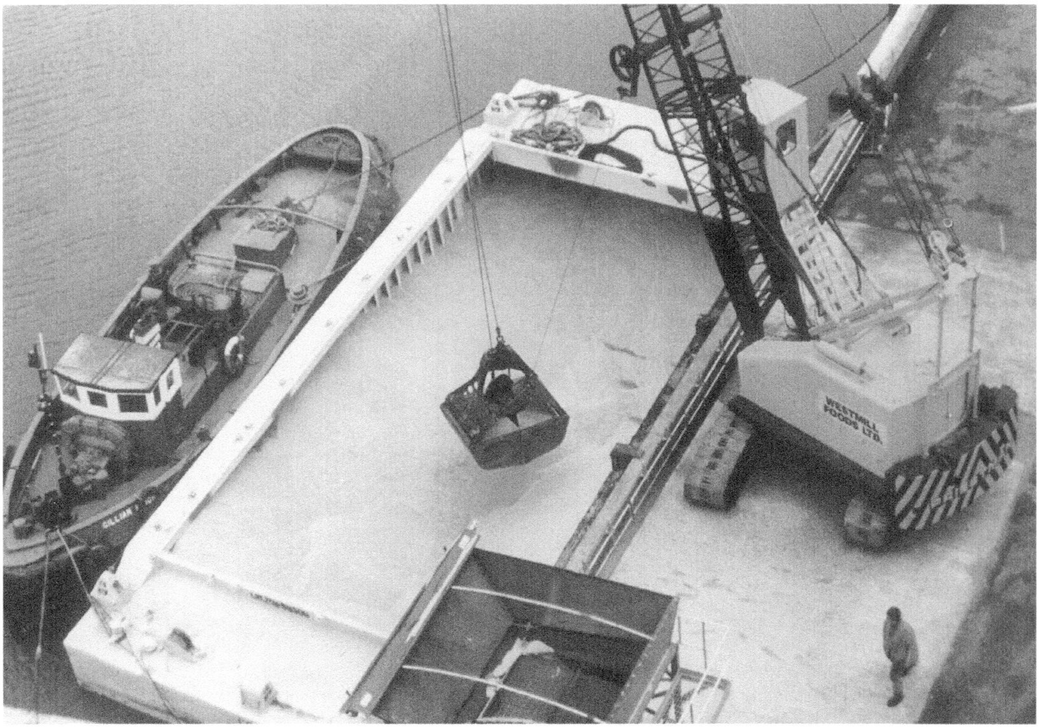

*Above:* Rice being discharged from a LASH barge at Selby in the twenty-first century. (Mike Brown)

*Right:* Victor Waddington always maintained that working two Sheffield size craft as a motor/dumb pair was the most efficient method of using the Sheffield size locks on the S&SYN above Doncaster. Here *Heritage* (see page 104), with wheelhouse deliberately collapsed is being used as a dumb vessel on the Denaby-Doncaster coal traffic as a pair prepare to leave Sprotbrough lock in 1978.

Waddingtons' dumb barge *No.40* (shown on page 62 being pull-towed), is here being pushed by *Northern King* (left). Both vessels, loaded with fluorspar, are waiting below Mexborough low lock in 2001, whilst Acasters' push tug *Little Kirkby* powers the 96ft x 17½ft *Selby Libra* down the S&SYN towards Goole, after discharging flurospar at Rotherham. (Mike Brown)

Acasters' *Selby Libra is* shown loading another cargo of imported fluorspar for Rotherham via a dumper truck on its return to Goole. (Mike Brown)

Graham Acaster welded three lighters (*River Star*, *P.O.E.M. 24* and *Twite*) together to make the 163ft long *River Star*, shown being handled by its tug *Little Shuva* on the river Trent at Besthorpe, prior to being loaded with aggregate in 2005. Rubbing strakes near the waterline indicate the joins. (John Noble)

The Belgian sea-going barge *Nieuwpoort*, shown loading 13,500 tons of coal for export at Immingham in 1970, is one of the largest push-towed craft ever to visit the Humber waterways. (Associated British Ports)

# Other titles published by Tempus

## Tugs and Towing Barges on the Humber Waterways
MIKE TAYLOR

Featuring the tugs and towing barges that have moved cargoes on the Humber's inland waterways from early in the twentieth century to the present day, Mike Taylor's descriptions of the relevant traffic movements are accompanied by illustrations from Lincolnshire, Nottinghamshire and Yorkshire.

978 0 7524 3804 7

## Tanker Barges on the Humber Waterways
MIKE TAYLOR

With a wide selection of illustrations interspersed with the recollections of men who worked on the waterways, this detailed book provides a history of the tanker barges that have moved liquid cargoes on the Humber's inland waterways from the early twentieth century to the present day and is a companion volume to *Tugs and Towing Barges on the Humber Waterways*.

978 0 7524 3921 1 8

## Shipping on the Humber  The North Bank
MIKE TAYLOR

This fascinating collection of images depicts the entire history of shipping on the river Humber. It features many illustrations and maps, accompanied by interesting and informative text.

978 0 7524 3116 1

## Shipping on the Humber  The South Bank
MIKE TAYLOR

Mike Taylor has collated a diverse selection of material to illustrate the history of shipping on the river Humber, using a variety of images and maps. and revealing the history of the growth and decline of the industry and the area.

978 0 7524 2780 5

If you are interested in purchasing other books published by Tempus, or in case you have difficulty finding any Tempus books in your local bookshop, you can also place orders directly through our website

www.tempus-publishing.com